BAIL OUT!

A POW'S STORY

Bill McFerren

Liberator Press

Bail Out! a POW's story

Edited by Published by Betty McFerren

Excerpts from *Rendezvous with Destiny* by John W. (Jack) Field, published by Phoenix Publishing, Canaan, NH, 1984

Cover and Book design: Nick Zelinger, NZ Graphics, www.nzgraphics.com

Library of Congress Control Number: 2005925233

ISBN: 0-9768897-0-6

First Edition, May 2005

Printed in the United States of America

Dedication

To Al Paris, Fyrtle Myrtle's copilot from the very beginning through her seventeenth mission, without whose encouragement (read: pushing, and prodding) this story would never have been finished. 1995, Bill, suffering from Parkinson's Disease, narrated the story to a secretary, Bill Boas, who took it down word for word, filling a loose-leaf binder with typed pages, including a gazillion letters. At that time I did not have the mental courage to attack the formidable task of pulling everything together in book form, nor, in all honesty, did I want to relive those painful years. Now, many years later, thanks to Bill's lifelong friend, Al Paris, who periodically said, "Betty, when are you going to get busy on that book?" I have gotten busy.

So, here it is, for better or for worse, but not without my eternal gratitude to you, Al. I understand now how true Bill's words were: "If Al had been on that last mission, we never would have been shot down!" (Al, in the copilot's place, with his forceful personality and wisdom, would have joined Bill in insisting that they lose no more time hanging around the target with Zeros only a hundred miles away.)

So, with profound appreciation I dedicate this book to Al Paris and the brave crew of Fyrtle Myrtle, and Bill would, too, were he here today.

Betty McFerren

The Crew of "Fyrtle Myrtle"

(Standing)

Copilot: Lt. Al Paris, Navigator: Lt. Bill McFerren,
Nose Gunner and Engineer: Tech Sgt. James DeGroat,
Radio Operator and Gunner: Tech. Sgt. Howard Sleighter,
Assistant Radio Operator and Waist Gunner: Sgt. Daniel Glendon,
Top Turret Gunner: Sgt. Louis Glavin,
Tail Gunner: Staff Sgt. James Lovett

(Squatting)

Radio and Gunner: Staff Sgt. John Lardin,
Bombardier: Lt. John Perry,
Pilot: Captain John Farrington

Contents

CLASS OF SERVICE

This is a full-rate Telegram or Cablegram unless its deferred character is indicated by a suitable symbol above or preceding the address.

WESTERN UNION

1204

SYMBOLS

DL=Day Letter

NT=Overnight Telegram

LC=Deferred Cable

NLT=Cable Night Letter

Ship Radiogram

A. N. WILLIAMS, PRESIDENT · NEWCOMB CARLTON, CHAIRMAN OF THE BOARD · J. C. WILLEVER, FIRST VICE-PRESIDENT

The filing time shown in the date line on telegrams and day letters is STANDARD TIME at point of origin. Time of receipt is STANDARD TIME at point of destination

33 S B 47 GOVT WUX WASHINGTON DC 407PM NOV 2

MRS BETTY C MCFERREN
P.O. 266
CORONA CAL

THE SECRETARY OF WAR DESIRES ME TO EXPRESS HIS REGRET THAT YOUR HUSBAND FIRST LTEUTENANT WILLIAM MCFERREN HAS BEEN REPORTED MISSING IN ACTION IN SOUTHWEST PACIFIC AREA SINCE TWENTY SIX OCTOBER IF FURTHER DETAILS OR OTHER INFORMATION OF HIS STATUS ARE RECEIVED YOU WILL BE PROMPTLY NOTIFIED.

ULIO THE ADJUTANT GENERAL

242P

THE COMPANY WILL APPRECIATE SUGGESTIONS FROM ITS PATRONS CONCERNING ITS SERVICE

Corona, California
V-Mail, November 3, 1943

My darling sweetheart,

I am writing because - Oh-darling, I do not believe the horrible news I received in a wire last night. It can't be true it can't it can't it can't - that's all. I just won't have it. You asked me what the anguish of childbirth was - I would rather endure that a thousand times more than one night like I spent last night, and instead fate will it that the childbirth shall only be once and there are a thousand nights.

No, no, no - Sweetheart, I don't believe it, and I'm writing to tell you so. You see I know you will get back to base, somehow, my navigator, and when you do, this letter will be waiting for you to tell you I know you are all right. See? Do not worry, my Sweet, as I am taking good care of Willie and he is great company to me. He with his great big toothless grin. He is so like you - the most perfect husband a woman ever had. You have made me know life at its very highest, and you will come back to me, Sweetie, I know you will. Always, Sweetheart, I am in love with you. Betty

Betty's Story

My world had just fallen apart. When that motorcycle pulled up in our gravel driveway, I felt a terrible apprehension that it was bringing something I wasn't going to like. When the dogs barked, I had only a few seconds left in my happy world before being plunged into unmitigated grief. The messenger handed me a Western Union envelope and roared away into the night.

MISSING IN ACTION! Wasn't that something that happened to other people? Missing in action in the 'Pacific Theater of War' (as it is so inappropriately called) Theater? Ugh! It was more like a boiling cauldron of witches' brew. Anyhow, the words 'missing in action in the Southwest Pacific' usually involve water, lots of it, deep and salty. Bill is a good swimmer, but... Was he wearing his Mae West? A thousand questions flooded through my mind.

The brief news had taken seven days to reach me—did they send it by carrier pigeon? It was many more days before letters from the Group arrived, giving me the sparsely available details. There had been eleven on board—ten regular crewmembers and a photographer. Five to eight parachutes had been reported. (Dear God, let it be eight.) Parachutes - PARACHUTES – do you mean a piece of flimsy white nylon was all that lay between my sweetheart and certain death if he were one of the lucky ones able to get out of the wreck?

What terror could force a man to jump into thin air, thousands of feet above land or sea, fumbling for the ripcord to release the canopy that would arrest his freefall and carry him toward a new unknown horror: gunfire or shark-infested water. God or lady Luck or whatever administrator of fate you believe in would have to protect him from being strafed by enemy fighters on the way down. Even the smartest man in the world would have no control there.

And yet—when faced with the alternative—the final moments of a burning and about-to-explode hunk of hot metal that had been a mighty aircraft, the decision to jump was certainly the lesser of the evils. At a time like that, you do what the experts have trained you to do. You jump. And pray. If you have time for prayer.

Nothing in my twenty-four years had ever remotely prepared me to deal with a blow like the one that arrived in a yellow envelope on a motorcycle that dark November night. The man I planned to spend the rest of my life with might be dead. And dead is forever. We had such a short time together. Was that all? Was his life over now?

Sleep refused to come that night. In the cold hard light of day, I began to assess the situation. Bill was very resourceful, very smart. I always told him he was the smartest man in the world. I learned so much from him. I was convinced that if he hadn't been killed outright, he would find a way to be in one of those parachutes. If captured, he would use his 'people skills' to placate the enemy enough to survive and come back to me and the baby son he had never seen.

My friends all said, "You're so brave not to lose hope." Heck, it didn't take bravery to believe what I wanted to believe. I could always face the worst if I had to, but I've never believed in borrowing trouble. It didn't cost any more to think that things would turn out as I hoped. I guess that's what is called being an optimist. Why suffer unless you absolutely have to? They're not giving any prizes for A-number-one sufferers.

Bravery? I'll tell you about bravery. Just what made that crew climb aboard Fyrtle Myrtle for each foray into they knew-not-what, knowing full well each flight could be their last, ending in some grisly, unimaginable way. If fate favored them with one more safe arrival home to be debriefed and to relax with a few drinks of welcome anesthesia, they still knew they would go through the whole thing all over again in another few days. Bill had done it 17 times before October 26. Now <u>that's</u> bravery.

Those twenty-three months that my beloved husband spent in various prison camps and that I spent waiting, not knowing if he were dead or alive, I lived and functioned, ate and slept, changed baby diapers—all pretty much without any feeling. It was two years of zombie-like existence. Our "little navigator" grew and, thrived; never having known his Daddy, he was blissfully unaware of what he was missing. At the war's end, the zero hour came for me. Waiting was over. Now I would find out if our son and I were among the lucky ones whose loved ones would soon be returning home to them. I was on pins and needles. We were without a phone in the beach town of San Clemente, California, in a house my folks planned for their retirement. A telephone was out of the question because there were no lines available along with new cars, gasoline, tires, nylons, sugar, Kleenex, and all the other wartime shortages. Pat and Paul Gilliland, retired military living nearby, invited me to use their phone number as a contact point.

Late on the afternoon of September 8, I was preparing dinner with my old schoolmate, Marion Minger who was visiting, when we were startled by a loud racket out in front. Someone was beating on the door, and then we heard Pat Gilliland screaming "He's in Manila!! He's in Manila!!" I remember that moment as though it were yesterday. The feelings of disbelief—I had hardly dared hope it might be true. I could scarcely breathe. We had won the lottery! All this and heaven too! What a mélange of emotions! Was this really happening or was I dreaming again? My joy was tinged with sadness for others whose news would not be good. From that moment on, life was a whirlwind of phone calls, arrangements, and celebration for young Bill and me.

Preface

Until I began the daunting task of putting my husband's story together, I had no idea how dormant those memories had become, only to be awakened like Chinese water flowers (those dried-up little paper nothings when dropped into a glass of water that suddenly blossom forth into colorful flowers). The fifty-four intervening years of our life together were so amply filled with multitudinous things—family, business, travel, fun together, squabbling together—that records, photos, letters, etc. from those tumultuous war years lay undisturbed, boxed up in our basement. Now, in reliving those days, I am once more made keenly aware of Bill's undying kindness and love of people. As I had hoped and prayed would be the case, that was a big part of what got him through those perilous POW days alive.

Daily reminders of deprivations suffered by Prisoners of War will always remain. Seeing Bill eat fried chicken gave me a twinge. He always cleaned every bit of meat from the bones just as he did with skimpy prison rations, though there wasn't much meat on bones there unless they were fish heads.

Later, the gusto and enthusiasm with which he lived life contributed to alcoholism. What actress Mercedes McCambridge once said in an AA meeting is so true: "You never know when you cross that line into alcoholism." Addiction is so treacherously easy to fall prey to, and so wrenchingly hard to defeat. When Bill understood the problems alcohol was causing for him and his family, he dug his heels in and with lots of help from the camaraderie of Alcoholics Anonymous, did what it took to give up drinking. Once he beat the problem, he was a far happier person (he had quit smoking years before that). His gratitude and devotion to AA became a big part of his last fifteen years.

In places, timeframes in this narrative may appear incongruous because facts that only surfaced after the war he includes as part of his story; but please keep in mind that Bill's insatiable curiosity prompted him to do extensive research to flesh out parts of the tale. I found in checking details with his copilot, Al Paris, that both men had similar and accurate memories.

Bill loved to fish. At the end, he had been in a coma for three days when he awakened enough to utter his last words, "I've been fishing all day and nobody could make me stop!" What a guy! He was almost 82.

CHAPTER I

BILL'S STORY:
COOKS AND BAKERS OR CALIFORNIA HERE I COME

In 1939 when Germany invaded Poland, a full-fledged war started incubating. England and Russia became involved and the Nazis were giving them all they could handle and then some. The United States, though not yet directly involved, was gearing up to help England with Lend Lease and supplies of food and material. I was working for the American Can Company in Chicago. A co-worker who had been sent to Washington to assist in procurement of food for the armed forces asked me to join him there. However, I found out that a requirement of the job he offered was that his assistant had to come from the ranks of the military.

Remembering that my father and my uncle had volunteered to serve in lighter than air observation balloons in World War I, it seemed only natural for me to join up, especially as I would be making a small contribution to better nutrition for the armed services. Besides, I had heard a rumor that Washington was full of single women.

Following the game plan devised by my American Can buddy in 1941, I quit my job and joined the army at Rockford, Illinois and after a short stint of basic training, I was shocked to learn that instead of the Valhalla in Washington that I dreamed of, my orders were for Fort Warren in Cheyenne, Wyoming. Compared to Washington, or even Chicago for that matter, Cheyenne turned out to be a social desert, windy and dusty—a small town in a state with a total population of only 250,000. There were probably more rattlesnakes and coyotes than people in Wyoming.

Noting that I had worked for American Can, and cans sounded like food, I was assigned to Cooks and Bakers School. During one class, the instructor went on and on about "veetamins" indicating to me that he didn't have much experience in nutrition. I questioned one point where I was sure he was wrong, and he tried to put me on the spot by asking, "Well, Private McFerren, where did you get all your information about nutrition?" I explained about my background with the Can Company. A Major who had been auditioning the class from the back row approached me afterwards and asked, "How would you like to be an instructor?"

Puzzled, I asked, "For what?"

"You could take that guy's place," he offered.

I didn't know how to respond to that so I sparred for time, saying, "I'd hate to take anybody's job away from him."

The Major told me, "Listen, you've gotta look after yourself," uncannily repeating the advice my father had given me when I left home.

So I became a nutrition instructor with a promotion to Sergeant and a whopping raise from $20 to $60 a month. By December 1941, I was supervisor of the Officer's Mess. One Sunday morning just before lunch, a radio broadcast interrupted regular programming with a startling announcement that Pearl Harbor had been bombed. They were not certain but thought it was by Japanese planes. I wasn't even sure where Pearl Harbor was, but the news sounded damn serious. I got a funny feeling in the pit of my stomach and wondered what that would mean for me.

The following Saturday night, when I went down to the Plains Hotel for a beer, that question was answered for me. I struck up a conversation with an Army Captain sitting next to me. Noticing that he was in the Air Corps, I mentioned that I had grown up near Chanute Field, which had been established in the early 1920s as one of the first Army Air Corps bases. My family and I knew a number of the military personnel stationed there including a Captain W. Cushman Farnum, who, with his wife, Louise, was then and would continue to remain a big part of my life. During our barstool chat, the Captain learned that I had graduated from Yale University. He offered, "I'm with the Air Corps recruitment board, would you by any chance be interested in joining up?"

"I'd do just about anything to get out of Cheyenne," I told him. "I'm freezing my ass off up here." Forgetting all about my desire to help improve the quality of food for the troops, not to mention providing company for all the lonely women in Washington, I enthusiastically plied him with questions about what his proposition had to offer. Satisfied that he had found a promising candidate, he diverted his attention to a more pressing concern. "Tell me, do you know any single girls here in Cheyenne?" he queried. I told him I knew one and she had a friend.

"Why don't you line those two up and we'll take them out dancing?" he suggested. I had to confess that idea was a bit out of my league at the moment, as I only had about $3 in my pocket.

"Look," he said, "I just got paid. Don't worry about the money—just get the girls." That settled, I called Shirley and we arranged to go dancing. In fact, the girls took us to a dance at the local country club, where we had a great time, winding up taking them home about 2 A.M.

After we dropped them off, my friend got back to his original purpose, "I'm serious about the Air Corps. With your background, you'd be a great pilot. Have you ever flown a plane?"

"My roommate at Yale had a Stearman and I flew it once," I bragged. Actually it was a very short flight and I was only at the controls for a few minutes.

"That's good enough," said he, "I've gotta give you a physical."

So after our evening of revelry, he gave me a cursory physical in the wee small hours. It's testimony to my youth and his lack of experience that I passed.

He told me, "I'm going to Omaha Monday and I'll take your papers with me. You'll hear from me within a week. The Air Corps has a priority call for eligible people, no matter what branch of the service they're presently in." I was on pins and needles. A week later a wire came ordering me to report to Minter Field in Bakersfield, California for air cadet training.

After a thirty-day leave spent living it up in my hometown of

Hoopeston, Illinois, I left for Bakersfield late in February 1942, only three months after the bombing of Pearl Harbor and one month before my 27th birthday.

"Yippee!" I thought, "Goodbye Wyoming! California here I come!"

CHAPTER 2

LAGUNA BEACH

After a short orientation period in Bakersfield, which was a desert-like area that looked suspiciously like Wyoming, I was transferred to Santa Ana Army Air Base for ground school. This was more like it. Los Angeles, Hollywood, and the Pacific Ocean were close. Things were looking up at last.

After countless hours of brain-busting classroom work relieved by an occasional dip in the cold salt water of the Pacific or a dash into Los Angeles on a weekend pass, it was time to fly at last.

I was transferred to Visalia Dinuba Air Base near Fresno, California, but as luck would have it, not for long. After six hours of flight instruction I was sent up for a check ride and washed out immediately. One problem was that the instructor asked me to do maneuvers I had not yet been taught. Using methods like this, he washed out 68% of the class, and earned the nickname "One Ride Porter." At this rate the Air Corps would be hard put to graduate enough pilots to fly the thousands of aircraft now in production. The brass got wind of the situation and a General descended upon the place, tore the staff apart, and replaced most of the flight instructors with better-qualified men.

However, my problems did not stop there. Tests revealed that I lacked depth perception, which spelled the end of my career as a pilot. I suddenly realized that I had wanted to be a pilot more than anything else in the world, and now it looked as though my dreams of flying had crashed and burned. It was the only time in the service that I cried my eyes out. Life was so unfair.

My new instructor, seeing how disconsolate I had become, said the chances were that poor depth perception would probably not be a problem in routine flying, but wingtip-to-wingtip formation required it to be one hundred percent. He asked about my mathematical skills, and said if I was any good at that, I might make an excellent navigator. This cheered me up because mathematics had always been easy for me. I applied for a transfer to navigation school.

The second time around at Santa Ana the rules were the same. Navigators said pilots were navigators with their brains blown out, and pilot trainees reversed the compliment, but on weekends most of us just went prowling for some fun.

Only months before, the attack on Pearl Harbor had brought a 180-degree turn around to the protocol of customs and proper manners as we had known them. I had been brought up by a New England mother who saw to it that I observed the mores of the day, whereby you had to be introduced to nice young ladies, but now that we were in all-out war, life went on fast forward. We seized the best the moment had to offer and improvised the rest. All we were sure of was today—you couldn't count on tomorrow, and time was of the essence.

We cadets could get a weekend pass to go and do whatever we wanted—at least as far as $75 a month would take us. Los Angeles was near and glitzy, so many of us took to visiting there almost every weekend. The first thing we did was look for a place to stay, and the second thing was to look for girls. One weekend my two buddies and I found a small hotel across from the ritzy Ambassador on Wilshire Boulevard (where suites cost around $100 a night). We got two bedrooms for three of us for $5. My friends had dates and I was the odd man out.

I told those smug dated-up guys, "I'm going to pick up the first good-looking girl that comes down the street."

They laughed and started making bets that I couldn't do it. I left and went out on Wilshire Boulevard. It wasn't long before a real good-looking girl came along and I stopped her, saying politely, "Pardon me, Miss, could you give me some information?" (The cadet uniforms were smart looking and always served to give a kind of reassurance.)

She hesitated, and I asked, "Could you tell me where I could find a nice girl who would like to go out tonight and have a good time?"

"Well..." she wasn't quite sure what I was leading up to. I supplied, "One like you..."

She smiled and said, "Well, it might be fun." I introduced myself and asked her name. We went across the street and had a drink at the Ambassador. Since money was in short supply, I suggested that we go back to my hotel where I had a bottle.

After a few more drinks and a lot of talk, she said, "Could I ask you a question?"

That seemed reasonable to me, and she continued, "Could I have one more drink before we go to bed?" I was somewhat taken aback, but as I said, it was wartime. Who was I to argue? So that was that and I went to Los Angeles the next three weekends until I learned she was getting serious and I wasn't. I certainly didn't want any more complications in a life scenario that had already seen enough ups and downs for one war.

I felt I needed a complete change of pace. I asked my barracks roommate, Horace "Goldie" Lund, "How would you like to go down to Laguna Beach this weekend?" Goldie had always loved the water, so that sounded good to him and we headed for Laguna, where we met two nice nurses in a bowling alley. Our team lost so we owed them a drink, but a serviceman couldn't buy alcohol until 6 P.M. It was about 4:30 then. My pretty partner said, "Why don't we go up to my house? I've got some booze." We took her up on it and had a drink at her house and were getting along just great when she asked the $64,000 question, "By the way, where are you guys staying tonight?" I told her we were going to have to find a place.

"If you'd like to stay here, I have an extra bedroom downstairs," she offered. Goldie and I thought the gods had smiled upon us for sure, but then she said "I've got a small problem. I'm caregiver for a disabled millionaire. I fix his dinner and put him to bed every night." Then she had a thought. "Why don't you boys have dinner and meet us afterward? There's a restaurant down on the beach that serves good seafood. It's called Las Ondas."

Dutifully Goldie and I went to Las Ondas and were studying the menu when a waitress came to our table. (It turned out to be Betty Garvey who was to become my wife!) I was captivated by her sparkling green eyes as I asked, trying any way I could, to strike up a conversation, "Which do you recommend, the Shrimp Creole or the French-fried Shrimp?"

She answered rather hurriedly, "I don't particularly care for shrimp, so I can't honestly say, but I'm sure they're both excellent."

I could see that approach wasn't going anywhere – I had to think fast and seeing a ring with a large blue-green stone on her finger, I seemed to remember once hearing a similar stone called a turquoise, so I took a chance, "Say, that's a beautiful turquoise you're wearing." As that seemed to interest her, I continued, "I love turquoise. I have a collection of over 200 of them." That was a bald-faced lie. I didn't own the first turquoise, but seeing that I had her attention, I continued brazenly on, "They're magical stones; I have several books on them."

Apparently I'd struck the right chord. Betty was serving dessert when I decided to see about a date, and asked if she would meet me after work.

"Thank you," she answered somewhat regretfully, "I wish I could but I already have a date." Of course I also had another date, but Betty and some ineffable mystery of the moment seemed more important. Goldie and I arranged to meet later and I moved to the bar to wait things out. I wondered if I'd lost my mind, to stand up a nice nurse for this waitress whom I knew not the first thing about except that she didn't like shrimp! After a while I saw another cadet come in as though looking for someone, and I guessed he might be her date, so I spoke to him asking if he might be looking for the girl wearing white shoes.

Surprised, he said he was, and asked, "Why? Do you know her?" I had some quick thinking to do so I improvised. "Yes, she's an old friend. I flew in tonight from Luke Field to see her, but apparently we must have gotten our signals crossed, darn it," I tossed the ball in his court.

He thought about it, then grudgingly capitulated saying he didn't want to stand in the way of renewing an old friendship.

That settled, I hung around the bar. Betty got off work and saw me and not her date. Smelling a rat, she asked me if I knew anything about it.

"I sent him packing," I told her.

She snapped, "You've got a lot of nerve!"

"You'd be surprised how much nerve I've got," I bragged.

She surveyed the situation for a moment and after adding it up, said reluctantly, "Looks like I'm stuck with you."

"You're not stuck," I assured her, "let's go dancing. We'll have fun, I guarantee you."

We ended up dancing all night at the Broiler and immediately discovered that Begin the Beguine was the favorite song for both of us. In a brash moment hoping to make a good impression, I told the band I'd buy them a drink every time they played it. They accommodated me by playing it several times—that great Artie Shaw arrangement—and I didn't even have enough money left for a hamburger! Betty had helped me spend it so she volunteered, "Tips were pretty good tonight. I'll lend you some." So I ended up borrowing from my future wife the first night we met. As I said before, there was a war on, you did what you had to do—who knew what tomorrow would bring?

Some strange electricity was taking place between us. We both sensed it. There didn't seem to be the usual game playing common to a developing relationship. Betty told me her best friend

Swingin' and Refuelin' In the South Pacific

Tom Nolan's Feb. 20 Leisure & Arts interview with Artie Shaw brought back memories of May 1943.

While stationed aboard the USS North Carolina en route from Pearl Harbor to Noumea, New Caledonia, Artie Shaw and his Navy band were passengers. After five days at sea, it became necessary to fuel the destroyers that were the anti-submarine screen. As they came alongside, they were greeted by the music of Artie Shaw and his band, made up of former professional musicians (Davey Tufts, Max Kominsky, etc.). The refueling operation took about four hours under the South Pacific sun.

They spent the next few days below deck being treated for severe sunburn, but they had provided a wonderfully unexpected treat for the crews of the ships.

James V. Grealish
Rear Admiral, USNR, (Ret.)
San Francisco

had gone to sleep driving and was killed the month before. She felt terrible about losing her friend but also felt a sense of anger because it was Mary Jeanne's second night without sleep. Working her way through college, Mary Jeanne held down two jobs in the summer relying on her boundless stamina to assign a low priority to sleep. The loss of her best friend and the pervading uncertainty of the war helped Betty decide to abandon the academic life even though she needed only one more year to get her degree in Home Economics. College simply did not seem relevant any more. It was September 1942 and the nation was still reeling from the dreadful sneak attack on Pearl Harbor. War in the Pacific was not going well and school got pushed aside. She took a job teaching sewing at the Singer Sewing machine company in Santa Ana and worked weekends at Las Ondas. She acknowledged that neither job was exactly vital to the war effort, but I assured her that boosting the morale of our fighting men was indeed a very necessary contribution. I'd already made my own decision in regard to the war effort so we had lots to talk about. We found that we had similar views, and strong ones at that, on almost everything!

I told her that since it was wartime, we had to skip the first four or five dates. There really was something to that—there simply wasn't much time as I was scheduled to transfer to Mather Field 500 miles north on Tuesday. It was now early Sunday morning.

I walked her home to a friend's place where she was spending the night, and we smooched a little on the steps. I tried to coax her down to the beach with a blanket, but she'd have none of that, though she did seem to like me pretty well. We agreed to meet for breakfast in the morning, and I hoped I'd have a bit more luck with her then, but I was wrong. When I got there, she introduced me to her friend's nine-year-old daughter. It was charming but not exactly what I had in mind.

Betty was living in Santa Ana so it didn't take much persuasion to get her to agree to meet me for a Coke at the base after work on Monday. Don't ask me why we picked the infirmary as a place to meet—probably because it was one place we both could find.

However I forgot one very vital thing: a civilian couldn't just enter the base at will, not with security beefed up after that submarine fired on Santa Barbara.

Monday, Betty arrived at the gate as agreed, but, of course, was refused entry. This stumbling block only strengthened her resolve to beat the situation. Stubbornly, hoping for some miracle, she refused to leave the gate house. Finally, the miracle happened. Her roommate, Mary Ann Castor, who worked at the base, drove through on her way home. The guard was tired of having Betty hanging around anyhow, so when Mary Ann vouched for her, he told her to go on through. Of course by this time I'd decided that I'd been stood up, and left the infirmary. Betty, finally on the base, went to the infirmary and figured she'd been stood up. She was walking forlornly back to the gate through a section not frequented by cadets when another miracle happened—she saw Goldie Lund and a friend coming down the street! Out of 3,000 cadets, the only one she knew was Goldie! She told me later, she grabbed him like a drowning person grabs a lifeline and screamed, "Goldie! Where's Bill?" He knew I'd gone to the PX so Betty and I did get together briefly. I got her address and left the next day for Sacramento.

Once there, I missed Betty terribly, and though our first encounters had been so short, I sensed that it wasn't your garden-variety, run-of-the-mill flirtation. I knew it mustn't stop there. I thought of those green eyes and wrote her a letter inviting her to come to Sacramento for a visit, and to make it more socially acceptable, suggested that she bring a friend for Goldie. Betty told me that she almost turned handsprings when she got my letter. She knew that she had to get to Sacramento somehow. Then fate took a hand at this point (as it had before). Betty received another letter, this one from Miss Struve, the Dean of Women at the University of California at Davis where she had spent her first three years. The letter said, "It has come to my attention that you are not planning to return to school to complete your senior year. I cannot urge you strongly enough to change your plans and complete your education. I know you will be very sorry if you do not." There were less than 100 girls at the University (it was an Ag school) and "Struvie" was close to all of them. Betty said it was as though the hand of God had picked her up by the scruff of the neck and whisked her back to school.

CHAPTER 3

WARTIME WEDDINGS

A couple of weeks later Betty arrived in Sacramento, accompanied by a close friend, Palma Jean Linville, a slim mahogany-haired young lady given to wearing pale pink cashmere sweaters. PJ had quit school along with Betty and was working in Sacramento. Goldie was immediately smitten.

Betty had registered for the fall semester at the University of California in Berkeley instead of her old stomping ground at Davis, because her required classes weren't given at Davis. However, Berkeley was only ninety miles from Sacramento so this still kept things in the realm of possibility; also there was frequent rail service between the two cities.

From that time on, the four of us were together every weekend with the exception of one when Betty had a date with an old college friend known affectionately as "Uncle Ellie," then a pilot flying for the Royal Canadian Air Force. (The RCAF took eligible men, who for one reason or another had been turned down by the U.S. Air Corps.) He was killed not long after in a crash in England.

That entire period from September 19, 1942, when we met, to January 2, 1943, when we were married, was the most intense and chaotic time of my life. I lived only to see Betty on weekends, and studied, flew, and just endured in between.

We exchanged lots of letters, and Betty saved every letter I ever wrote her, both from Sacramento and overseas. I saved hers, too, and they went to Australia with me but were lost when I failed to come back from our eighteenth mission. She said that she never threw away even one of my letters because it seemed she would be throwing away a little piece of me.

I had expected upon graduation at the first of the year to be retained stateside as an instructor, but proving that you can never count on anything in wartime, our entire class got orders for combat.

Late in December I learned that I was assigned to join a squadron of the 380th Bombardment Group presently forming up at Davis-Monthan Field in Tucson, Arizona. I asked Betty if she would go with me, not mentioning the subject of marriage.

Betty took care of that. It was put up or shut up time. She said very pointedly, "Just what would be my status?"

"Well," I said, "I guess I'll have to marry you!" I had already hinted around pretty graphically in little ways, such as drawing monograms using McF as her last initial, so she didn't exactly say, "Oh, this is so sudden!"

We arranged to be married in San Francisco and that weekend I took the train down to meet her Aunt and Uncle who were pleased as punch to be stand-ins for her parents who lived in Southern California. Clayton Garvey had been in law practice in San Francisco for many years—he was a perfect delight and so was her Aunt Sadie. Childless, they were immensely enjoying their roles as 'family' to our romance.

When the day came that we planned to be married, it had to be postponed because there was a California law requiring a three-day interval between the time the license was applied for and its actual issuance. (Something to do with a Wasserman Test, I believe.) Further, it was okay for either the bride or groom to apply for the license, but both had to appear together to sign and pick it up. Betty went down to the San Francisco City Hall, filled out the papers and paid the $2, but we still had to appear together to pick it up.

I was in class one day when a corporal came in and whispered something to the instructor who chuckled and said "Cadet McFerren, stand up." So I stood at attention while he said, "There's a young lady at the gate who says she has a wedding license for you to sign." That just about broke up the class. Flustered but happy, I signed.

Saturday, January 2, 1943, was a very big day for me. After flying my final hours early, I received my coveted silver wings and my commission as a Lieutenant in the United States Army Air Corps. (Later, the word 'Army' was dropped and it became simply 'Air Force.') We had one more hurdle, that of obtaining the wedding license together. I asked for a 24-hour pass but it was refused because orders had been cut to leave the next day.

I said to myself "Screw 'em!" and headed for San Francisco, going AWOL in the process, probably not the best attitude for a newly commissioned officer in wartime, but as I said before, you did what you had to do. That evening I got off the train in Oakland and hopped aboard the ferry for San Francisco, where Betty and her Uncle picked me up. Then at Clayton and Sadie's house, I met my future father- and mother-in-law, Stanley and Madeline Garvey, and Betty's brother, Stan, for the first time. They seemed to approve, but the hard part was ahead. We still didn't have the certified wedding license because it was locked up in the San Francisco City Hall and it was now 7:30 Saturday night. However lady luck had been our constant companion since the night we met and she was not about to desert us now. Clayton, through years of legal work was well acquainted with the San Francisco City Clerk who had a key to the City Hall. Wartime security mandated a citywide semi-blackout, called a "dim out" and we drove slowly through darkened streets using only parking lights.

When we reached the clerk's house, he was bathing his baby, but he came with us anyway, heading for a side entrance of the City Hall. We walked through dark cavernous hallways using only a flashlight till we came to the Marriage License Bureau where we were finally able to sign together in his presence. We drove back through miles of darkened streets to the Ingleside Episcopal Church where the Reverend Veazie, Betty's folks with her brother Stan, and her Aunt Sadie patiently waited. As I said before, the country just couldn't do enough for its fighting men. That certainly made me feel good. Our marriage vows seemed almost anticlimactic after all we'd been through together, with dogged determination finally prevailing!

Sadie and Clayton had a three-tiered wedding cake for us with a little soldier and his bride perched on top. It had been in cold storage since the aborted wedding date the previous week. The cake ended up in a Brown and Foreman whiskey box accompanying us on the next leg of our exciting journey, and would soon be devoured by my classmates.

In the confusion and haste, I had forgotten to arrange for a place to stay that night. I called for a room at the St. Francis but they were overbooked so we crossed Powell Street to the little Hotel Stewart, which also did not have a room. We were in a quandary and it must have showed because the manager came out and asked, "By chance, did you kids just get married?" He had a private room there but didn't live in it, so he asked if we would like to have it. Boy, would we! It had been a long stressful day from early morning, flying, catching trains and ferries etc. What a relief to find a place to rest and be alone. And to put the frosting on the cake, he said because it was our wedding night there would be no charge.

Betty went into the bathroom to freshen up and when she came out, I was snoring, fully clothed on the bed! The next thing I knew it was 8:30 A.M. and I had slept my entire wedding night! She said, "Sweetie, you looked so peaceful, I didn't have the heart to wake you." Problems were ahead. I called my other roommate, Harry Long, who said ominously, "Bill, you're in trouble. The duty officer (who was a real shit) is going to have you court-martialed for going AW0L." We scrambled to catch the next train to Sacramento, wondering why it seemed life was a kind of obstacle course.

Luckily, Captain Stadham, a friend, was on duty. Although he was a commissioned officer, he had gone through navigation school and graduated with me. All ninety three of us newly commissioned officers including Captain Stadham were due to take the train for Tucson in a couple of hours, but I didn't have my transfer papers since they were being withheld by that obstructionist Captain who intended to see that I was court-martialed. I was in a state of near panic because my whole career and our married life together seemed at stake—I had to get on that train. When Captain Stadham found out about it, he told me, "Bill, you and Betty go on down to the station, keep your mouth shut, and let me handle this."

I had no idea how he planned to handle it, and as I reflect back on it, I don't think he did either, but we just stood around, hoping.

I heard him say on the phone to the other Captain, "Bring McFerren's papers down to the station." He told me afterwards that his order had been refused by the other with the curt statement, "McFerren was AW0L and that calls for a court-martial."

As I said before, lady luck was still by my side. Captain Stadham asked the date of the other's commission. Talk about tense moments! His date was three weeks newer than Stadham's, meaning that Captain Stadham outranked him by three weeks! My savior bellowed, "You're not taking him to any hearing! Damn it, give me those papers!" Relief flooded over me, but we still weren't on the train together. I asked my Captain if I could take Betty on the train with me, and his answer was, "Well, according to regulations, you're entitled to a lower berth. If you can get her in it, you can take her with you." That was the easiest assignment yet.

There were eight other married couples on those three Pullman cars and one as yet unmarried couple who didn't have the necessary release from the bride's parish priest. Willie Mee and his wife and Betty and I made it our highest priority to somehow get Helen and Jerry properly married as soon as we reached Salt Lake, where we would be for the better part of a day.

We located a priest who was willing to help, using the rest of us as witnesses. He asked, "Is there anyone who has known this young lady for at least two years and can verify that she has never been married?"

When no one else responded, Betty sensing catastrophe about to strike, spoke up, "I have."

After the brief ceremony, it was time to fill out some papers. The priest (being a mischievous sort?) asked Betty to play secretary. Betty suddenly realized that she didn't know her old friend's last name.

The padre wisely said nothing about this strange situation.

Immediate problems behind us, the rest of the trip on the troop train containing ninety-three navigators and nine wives was a memorable honeymoon. We didn't worry about tomorrow—never even thought of it. We'd learned not to. Life recently had been precarious enough. A continuous poker game went on until the owner of the berth where it was held got tired and wanted to go to bed. The game would break up then until after breakfast, when it began again with renewed vigor.

On the next leg to Tucson, the train paused for twenty minutes at Las Vegas, which, in those days, was more or less of a whistle stop. Mostly less. However, even then Las Vegas did have gambling and it did have whisky. The train had barely screeched to a stop before it completely emptied of passengers, as though a giant vacuum cleaner had sucked them all out. There was only one dilapidated, run-down street about a block long and a few tawdry gambling houses—you couldn't exactly call them casinos. I bought a bottle, and upon returning to the train an MP said, "I'm sorry, Lieutenant, but you can't take liquor on the train." I quickly handed the bottle to Betty to whom military rules didn't apply, and we pulled out of the station well-supplied.

At Davis Monthan Field, something new had come up. We were supposed to train for battle over Europe, but General Douglas MacArthur had gone to Washington and convinced President Roosevelt that if we didn't get more support in the Pacific, Australia would go down the tubes. While the brass pondered this problem, our Group continued its training for whatever destination.

Available hotel rooms were practically non-existent, so Jerry and Helen Kopecky and Betty and I shared one. Jerry developed a medical problem that kept him out of the air, so while I flew, Betty soaked in the bathtub reading "For Whom the Bell Tolls" to allow our roommates a little privacy. When water in the tub got too cold, the privacy came to an end.

We were now part of the fledgling 380th Bomb Group, soon to be known as the "Flying Circus," and though we didn't know it then, we were destined to fly B-24 Liberators in the South Pacific. The Group consisted of four squadrons numbered 528 through 531, each squadron having nine planes. I was assigned to the 530th.

The air was full of excitement along with some apprehension. We were at last entering the great unknown. War was suddenly much closer.

CHAPTER 4

OFF TO MAKE THE WORLD SAFE FOR DEMOCRACY

Believe it or not, in the late 1930s history tells us that there were only about thirty qualified four-engine aircraft pilots in the country. By the war's end, that number had reached 15,000, and American manufacturing had made an incredible turnaround and started building airplanes and other military materiel like there was no tomorrow.

New automobiles became a thing of the past. Values of used cars skyrocketed. For example, Betty's brother had paid $125 for a Plymouth coupe before the war. It doubled in price to $250 by 1943, and shortly after the war Betty and I sold it for $425! Civilians were issued ration cards with stamps attached that could be spent for meat, sugar, three gallons of gasoline per week, tires, shoes, and cigarettes. Purchases of scarce goods were limited to the number of 'points' on your ration card. Almost everything was scarce—nylons, Kleenex, you name it. The military had first call.

Colonel William Miller, a Captain with American Airlines, answered his country's urgent plea for experienced multi-engine pilots. He assumed command of the 380th Bomb Group. Miller was one tough cookie and we had a lot of respect for him. He wouldn't ask anyone to do anything he wouldn't do—only catch was, there wasn't anything he wouldn't do! While we were training at Biggs Field in El Paso, Texas, he spotted a weakness in the way the slender 'Davis' wing was attached to the body of a B-24 and reported it to Consolidated Aircraft, manufacturer of the airplane. Getting the brush-off, our dauntless Colonel upped the ante and, using a few choice expletives, told them that if anyone had

UNITED STATES OF AMERICA
OFFICE OF PRICE ADMINISTRATION

586699 EE

WAR RATION BOOK No. 3

Void if altered

NOT VALID WITHOUT STAMP

Identification of person to whom issued: PRINT IN FULL

Betty McFerren
(First name) (Middle name) (Last name)

Street number or rural route P.O. Box 266

City or post office Corona State Calif.

AGE	SEX	WEIGHT Lbs.	HEIGHT Ft. In.	OCCUPATION

SIGNATURE Betty McFerren
(Person to whom book is issued. If such person is unable to sign because of age or incapacity, another may sign in his behalf.)

WARNING
This book is the property of the United States Government. It is unlawful to sell it to any other person, or to use it or permit anyone else to use it, except to obtain rationed goods in accordance with regulations of the Office of Price Administration. Any person who finds a lost War Ration Book must return it to the War Price and Rationing Board which issued it. Persons who violate rationing regulations are subject to $10,000 fine or imprisonment, or both.

OPA Form No. R-130

LOCAL BOARD ACTION

Issued by .... (Local board number) (Date)

Street address ....

City .... State ....

.... (Signature of issuing officer)

INSTRUCTIONS

1 This book is valuable. Do not lose it.

2 Each stamp authorizes you to purchase rationed goods in the quantities and at the times designated by the Office of Price Administration. Without the stamps you will be unable to purchase these goods.

3 Detailed instructions concerning the use of the book and the stamps will be issued. Watch for these instructions so that you will know how to use your book and stamps. Your Local War Price and Rationing Board can give you full information.

4 Do not throw this book away when all of the stamps have been used, or when the time for their use has expired. You may be required to present this book when you apply for subsequent books.

Rationing is a vital part of your country's war effort. Any attempt to violate the rules is an effort to deny someone his share and will create hardship and help the enemy.

This book is your Government's assurance of your right to buy your fair share of certain goods made scarce by war. Price ceilings have also been established for your protection. Dealers must post these prices conspicuously. Don't pay more.

Give your whole support to rationing and thereby conserve our vital goods. Be guided by the rule:

"*If you don't need it,* DON'T BUY IT."

16—82299-1 ☆ U. S. GOVERNMENT PRINTING OFFICE : 1943

the guts to go up with him, they would put on parachutes and he would shake the wings right off the damn plane. No one volunteered, and Consolidated gave up and agreed to the necessary modifications. You gotta love a guy like that.

Major Fred Miller was another with multi-engine qualification who went to work as our Squadron Commander whipping us into shape as airworthy crews. On an early training flight out of El Paso, I happened to be his navigator. Under overcast skies and poor visibility, instruments told me that if we continued on our present course and altitude, it wouldn't be long before we plowed into a 12,000 foot peak in the Rocky Mountains. I called this to his attention, but the Major, with all his experience, wasn't about to take a correction from a green 2nd Looey, and remained on course. I reviewed my calculations, and returned to the flight deck wearing my parachute. "Major," I said emphatically, "either we change course or gain at least 2,000 feet or I'm bailing out!"

Miller, seeing I was dead serious, decided to humor me with a change in altitude. Moments later he looked down through a break in the clouds.

"Holy shit," was all he said seeing a peak a few hundred feet below. That flight was the beginning of the enduring friendship and respect we shared from then on.

During training at Biggs Field our ten-man crew welded into a team that would stay together and function smoothly all through combat. Crews were intended to be permanent, since teamwork and trust were critical components of successful missions. Many flight personnel went over as replacements and had to integrate into their jobs with strangers. Our crew was very fortunate in being able to remain together from its very inception at Biggs Field. John Farrington was our Captain, Al Paris our copilot, John Perry, bombardier, and I was navigator, Tech Sergeant James DeGroat, engineer and nose gunner, Tech Sgt. Howard Sleighter, radio operator, Staff Sgt. John Lardin, radio and gunner, Sgt. Daniel Glendon, assistant radio operator and waist gunner, Staff Sgt. James

Lovett, tail gunner, and Sgt. Louis Glavin, top turret gunner—every one of them capable, gutsy and dependable.

Under Fred Miller's rigorous tutelage, our 530th squadron was one of the best-trained squadrons in the Group. At times, there was grousing about how tough 'Fearless Freddie' was but when push came to shove and the grim realities of war were upon us, I know we all realized how valuable his stiff discipline had been.

Missions lasted anywhere from two to eight hours, some of them over the bombing range at Alamogordo, New Mexico, which lay about an hour north of Biggs Field. On one night flight at about 5,000 feet starting the approach to the bombing range, as is customary, Bombardier John Perry took command ten miles from the target, directing the final approach. About thirty seconds before the bombs were to be released on the lighted target, I noticed something strange going on down there. I tapped John Perry on the shoulder and said, "Hey, John, did you ever see cars driving in and out of a target?" People gassing up at that filling station will never know how close they came to being on the receiving end of some five-pound practice bombs!

Life at Biggs Field was more or less an eight-hour job. After briefly sharing a room in Tucson with Jerry and Helen Kopecky, Betty and I were lucky to find what must have been the last vacant furnished apartment in El Paso. My ever-resourceful bride set up housekeeping by dint of several trips to Woolworth's for kitchen and bath supplies. Having known each other for only four months, we found that married life involved many new responsibilities. That wonderful honeymoon was made all the more piquant by its inevitable brevity. Ours was certainly not your storybook honeymoon on some tropical shore, but neither of us would have had it any other way. Our country had been attacked and Betty and I were just proud to be a part of its defense. We simply accepted whatever came and made the best of it.

Juarez, Mexico, just across the Rio Grande, was exciting, accessible, and cheap. That's where an enterprising waiter introduced us to Tequila Daisies one hot Saturday afternoon. The Daisy was a very smooth mixture of tequila, lime juice, and grenadine, and, as I recall, cost about 25 cents. Having consumed three of them, we walked out into the sun and just about passed out.

There are other memories of El Paso. One day I was walking along the flight line and paused by a jeep to shield me from the wind while I lit a match. The match kept blowing out and a hand from the jeep proffered a Zippo lighter. The hand belonged to Captain Clark Gable of recent "Gone With the Wind" fame. He was now a gunnery officer training B-17 crews, having left Hollywood glitz behind to contribute to the war effort. He was a regular guy—just 'one of the boys' during happy hours at the O Club (Officer's Club).

Around March 1, the 380th moved to Lowry Field in Denver, Colorado, to fly long missions throughout the western United States, Rocky Mountains, and the Pacific Ocean. We learned about the jet stream on one high altitude flight at about 30,000 feet when we accidentally entered it and were carried way off course over Iowa before anybody realized what was happening. The jet stream is a swift river of air that can vary in width, altitude, and location, but always flows west to east. It can be a very narrow slice of atmosphere only 2,000 feet wide at altitudes of 30,000 to 50,000 feet. It is not turbulent, just swift, so it can be very deceiving if you fly in it. Aviation only became aware of these meandering rivers of air with the advent of very high altitude flying during World War II.

A trip to California put us in to March Field near Riverside. An amusing incident there shows how old friendship can trump military protocol. One of the old Chanute Field crowd, whom I knew when I was growing up in Illinois, was a young Lieutenant—Sam Connell. At March Field, I was surprised to see Sam coming down the path and I greeted him like I always used to, "Hey, Sam, Baby!" We threw our arms around one another. Then I noticed the star on his shoulder and the officer with him reproved me, "Lieutenant, you don't call the General 'Sam, Baby!'" Since we were in public, he was right, but Sam eased the situation by saying, "This guy can."

Far more improbable than my chance encounter with General Connell was what happened to my copilot, Al Paris. Al and a couple of buddies took off after work for San Bernardino to stir up a little fun. As they were waiting for a traffic light to turn green, there were three girls in a convertible beside them also waiting for the light. Bottom line: back at March Field I was sleeping soundly when I felt someone shaking me and heard Al shouting, "Bill! Bill! I just met the girl I'm going to marry!" And he did just that.

We, of course, had to fly back to Denver the next day, but that didn't deter a guy like Al. He carried on a romance with Mickey via telephone and U.S. mail, and the next time he saw her was during the Group's six-day leave prior to overseas duty when she stepped off a plane in Minneapolis, Al's home town, to be married. Did such an incredible romance last? You bet it did. They spent 35 years together and raised three fine children. Sadly, Mickey died of cancer in 1978. Al is now married to his lovely wife, June, and retired in 1980 as vice president of Safeco Title Insurance. (Editor's note: Al is now 85 and, as the financial writers like to say, "lean and mean" and plays a lot of golf.)

At Lowry there were lots of playful times at the O club and other spots. Betty remembers a gala farewell dinner dance at the Brown Palace as our time at Lowry was winding down—everyone was having a fine time and Major Miller kept poking a finger at me and saying "laugh, Bill," because I was blessed with such an infectious belly laugh.

The thing Betty, a California girl, remembers most about that night was hearing cold, dry snow squeak underfoot.

Major Jack Bratton was in command of the 530th Squadron. He was a wonderful guy and a close friend to this day. He and his wife were staying at the Westward Ho Motel where we were, also. One time when he had to fly and I didn't, he asked me to meet his father who was due to arrive that afternoon from Tennessee. Jack said his pappy wasn't used to big city ways and might need a bit of assistance. I arranged for a car and drove down to the railroad station looking for a slight man who might appear somewhat scared and confused, according to Jack. When passengers departed from the train, I saw someone who fit that description carrying one huge suitcase and one little zipper bag. I asked if he were Jack Bratton's father.

"Yep, sure am," he grinned and set his bags down. I introduced myself and explained the game plan to him. I started to pick up the large bag and I could hardly lift it!

He warned me,"Be mighty careful with that bag, son,"

When we got to the Westward Ho, I horsed the big bag in and he told me,"Put it down real gently, please, I want to show you something,"

He opened that big bag and it was full of nothing but Jack Daniels bourbon! He explained, "I hated to have Jack go overseas with nothing but that lousy Yankee whiskey to drink." He gave me a pint of that nectar of the gods and then proceeded to regale us with stories of young Jack growing up in Tennessee.

Training flights out of Lowry continued throughout the month of March. In the first week of April we were told to send our wives home as the Flying Circus was heading for Topeka, Kansas, to pick up our brand new 24s. We already had a name for ours—Fyrtle Myrtle—because three of the crew wives were expecting, and Myrtle rhymes with Fyrtle. Other sassy names carried into battle by the 380th birds, and frequently to the bottom of the sea, were Sizzlin' Sue, Male Call, and Miss Giving, along with lots of first-class nose art.

Betty and most of the other wives ignored the orders to go home and became 'camp followers' at the Jayhawk Hotel in Topeka. Crews were confined to base, but by hook or by crook, it was sometimes possible to get a pass to go off base for a few hours. Lacking a pass, many just went over the fence and headed for the Jayhawk. One very early morning there were so many of us coming back to base, we formed up ranks and marched in!

Major Miller found out about my nightly sojourns and informed me that I'd be walking tours (an ignominious punishment for an officer) if he caught me doing it again.

Topeka was a dry town. I had two bottles of bourbon and offered

Nose Art

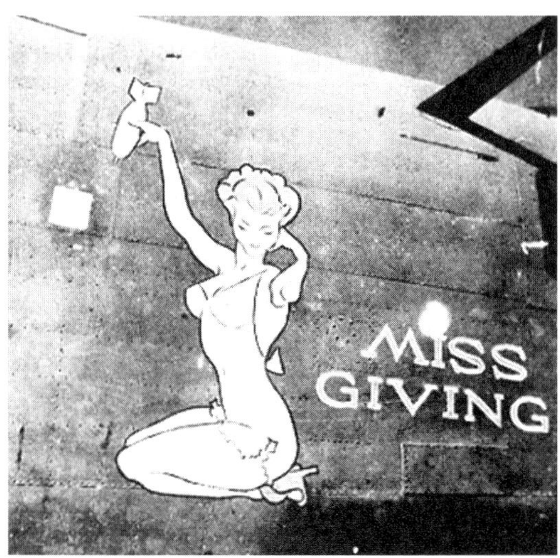

Left:
Captain Jack Bank's *Miss Giving* returned to Fenton with one engine out, low on ammunition and so short on fuel that he ordered the crew to put on parachutes in case they ran out. They touched down with one engine flat empty and only 10 minutes in the others. They shot down four fighters and sank one ship. (Note bullet holes.)

Right:
Arrow points to bullet hole in Lt. Bob Dunseth's 100 mission *Puss & Boots.*

Left:
Loe Dally's *Beautiful Beast's* nose art

one to the base Master Sergeant who asked "Do I have to kill for it?"

"No, but how's about some passes?" I answered. He asked how many I needed.

Never having been bashful, I suggested hopefully, "About fifty should do it."

To my delighted surprise, he agreed and I found myself custodian of fifty passports to family happiness. Ironically, Betty reported to me soon thereafter that Jane Miller, the Major's wife, had just checked in at the Jayhawk and was, of course, expecting to see him. Freddie learned about it and asked the Sergeant for a pass only to learn to his dismay, I'm sure, that I had all we were going to get. After his remark about walking tours, the last thing he ever wanted to do was ask me for a pass. But he had to visit his wife and so he came to see me. I smiled, handed him two passes, and didn't say one word!

Finally came the evil day signaling that the end of our honeymoon was near. We received orders for a six-day leave, after which we were to fly our new plane to Hamilton Field located across the Golden Gate from San Francisco, for immediate deployment to Australia. Betty and I spent a blissful six days leave in Hoopeston, Illinois, with my family.

Parting was bittersweet as the great unknown loomed ahead, but duty called and I headed back to Topeka. Betty already had planned to spend another week or two with my family. I wrote the following letter to Betty while I had the opportunity stateside. Little did I suspect the surprise that fate had in store for us!

April 25, 1943

Betty darling,

This is in a hurry so pardon my scribbling. I talked to your mother today but was unable to contact Clayton and Sadie, tried several times.

Darling, it was wonderful to talk to you the other night. I love you with all my heart, and I'll never be happy until we are together again—however, I realize we must make the best of a trying situation and with faith, love, and hope, I know we will be reunited again. No one could be cruel enough to part us now, when we have so much to look forward to. You have been everything to me a wife could be, and never will I forget the last rapturous months we spent together. With all the obstacles to our being together—the first day we got here Fred Miller asked me what plane you were arriving on—I might have seen you, but I think it was best as it was. My family so enjoy having you there, and I can't be too selfish I guess. I am as acclimated to the idea of leaving now as I ever could be, and we really got pretty good breaks as it was. One is inclined to forget the good things the fates throw your way and only remember the bad.

We have been very busy here, and I have been rushed every minute. I can't tell when I am leaving, but darling, when my letters start you will know. I tried to think as you told me Friday, but all that happened was I fell out of bed that night. My Sweet, all I have to do is close my eyes and I see your face before me. I love your picture so darn much and give it a kiss at least four times a day. I have only one ambition at present, and that is to come back to you.

I never knew how sweet life could be until you came into my life, and always, darling, always my heart and thoughts will be with you, whatever the outcome may be. Let's have faith as you say, and I know I will come back to you, my darling, my sweet. Roebury is going to drop you a note one of these days, after the veil of censorship has been removed....He, Sam Poon, and Lippincott and I played three rubbers of bridge till 12 pm last night. Willie did OK.

Darling, I hate to end this short, but I have no more time. All my love, all my thoughts, everything I have is yours, forever and ever.

Your loving, Bill.

P.S. Hello Muddy and Daddy, Marge and Pat. I love you all and miss you like hell. Always, Bill.

The next day we had orders to proceed with a 2,400 mile over-water flight to Hickam Field, Hawaii, first stop on our way to Australia. We departed early evening, but a few hours into the flight, trouble in the number I engine developed and it had to be shut down. Apparently the oil supply for the hydraulic system that changes pitch of the props had leaked out and John couldn't feather the prop. (When an engine is shut down, you have to 'feather' its prop so it slices through the air instead of remaining in flight pitch and presenting drag.) Sometimes John could get the dead prop to 'feather' and slice harmlessly through the air, but every half hour or so it would come back to flight pitch and 'windmill' creating a real control problem for the pilots. John asked me if I thought we could make it to Hawaii. As we were not quite halfway, I told him I'd a whole lot rather return to Hamilton. He radioed the field and they concurred completely as it would be much easier and faster to replace an engine there. We made a U-turn and I gave him a course back to Hamilton. An amazing thing was that all this time, the dials continued to read "All's well."

The auto pilot wouldn't work with one engine shut down, and Farrington and Paris did one helluva job keeping the plane in trim and on course. The two of them had to stand on the rudder pedals all the way.

When we finally neared the field, the tower told us to circle for half an hour as they were sending off a flight of twin engine B-25s while there was a 20-knot tailwind that the 25s needed for the 2,400-mile trip to Hawaii. We weren't too long on gas ourselves. John and Al were exhausted from fighting the disabled engine, but they started circling as directed when suddenly the dead engine's prop began windmilling again. That did it. John radioed the tower to clear the decks, we were coming in. At about 500 feet and the same distance from the runway, he dropped the landing gear. Just then the ailing prop froze in normal flight pitch. That sudden extra drag dropped us in seconds to about 50 feet off the water. Farrington pulled up the landing gear and pushed the throttles on the three working engines past the red line, which gave us just enough lift to clear the end of the runway. He quickly dropped the gear again and we touched down to an audible sigh of relief from everyone. Farrington and Paris had done an admirable job of airmanship!

After being assigned quarters, everyone went straight to bed for a well-earned rest except me. I was thinking about Betty and couldn't sleep. Early in the morning I headed for the shop where I knew the maintenance crew chief would come on duty to assess Myrtle's problem. When the first one showed up and looked her over, I asked him how long it would take to get the plane ready to fly.

He told me, "If we're lucky, it should be ready in about a week."

I rushed to a phone to call Betty in Hoopeston. My mother answered and was, of course, overjoyed at my safe return to California, but when she understood that I wanted Betty to fly to San Francisco, she switched to mother mode and said, "Well, Bill, Betty's three months pregnant and you know she really shouldn't be flying like that, and you're going to have to leave soon anyway. Why not forget it and let her stay here?"

I didn't mince words. "Muddy, she's my wife and I want her here."

I asked her to put my father on the line. He understood and was able to get a reservation on a United Airlines DC-3 out of Chicago for points west in about two hours. Daddy always did drive fast and they made it in time. There was only space available as far as Des Moines but she took it, hoping for a break. The 21-passenger plane made at least four or five more stops and each time Betty was lucky and got back on, until her luck ran out when they reached Las Vegas, the last stop. The plane was completely booked and Betty had to improvise. She talked her way onto the plane through the courtesy of a UAL Captain who was deadheading back to San Francisco. He gave Betty his seat and crammed himself into the cabin with the pilots. Lady luck had not deserted us!

This was the surprise that fate had in store for us. We stayed with Sadie and Clayton for one glorious, rapturous week of dining, dancing, sightseeing, and just being together without a care in the world in enchanted San Francisco, which still is to me the most exciting, romantic city I know. Sadie and Clayton's friends had parties for us—we were literally king and queen for a day! We were becoming pros at just living for the moment without a thought of what might lie ahead.

Finally I received word that that Myrtle was ready to fly. I got orders to report that afternoon to make a second attempt at crossing the Pacific. Betty and I rode a bus from Sadie and Clayton's place in the Ingleside district to the corner of 19th Avenue and Sloat Boulevard where I kissed her goodbye and transferred to a bus headed north across the Golden Gate Bridge. Though we both realized it would be a long time before we would see each other again—maybe never—little did I know that it would be two and a half lonely, bitter, miserable years till I saw that Golden Gate Bridge again.

Living it up in San Francisco's International Settlement during our free week off.

(Top photo, left to right) Tech. Sgt. James DeGroat, Staff Sgt. John Lardin, Staff Sgt. James Lovett, Tech Sgt. Howard Sleighter.

(Bottom photo) Howard Sleighter and John Lardin

Thanks to Betty Farrington and Al Paris for this and others to follow.

CHAPTER 5

ON TO AUSTRALIA - AGAIN

May 4, 1943, we again left California for Hickam Field, Hawaii, across 2,400 miles of open sea with some pretty scary recent memories following us. This would be the acid test of my navigational know-how. I was nervous to say the least. Thankfully, we had been put through such rigorous training before being certified competent to take this awesome four-engine beast with her crew of ten safely through whatever Mother Nature and the Japs could throw at us! In those days, navigation depended on sighting the sun or stars and landmarks, if you were not over open sea and weather permitted. You transposed those points into lines of position on a chart. Since there are no landmarks between the U.S. and the Hawaiian Islands, a one degree error multiplied by 2,400 miles could mean missing the destination by as much as 40 miles. It was easy to make an error in the extensive calculations needed. We didn't have the advantage then of even a $5.95 Wal-Mart calculator that every school kid takes for granted today. All math had to be worked out by hand on paper with the help of a kind of circular slide rule. Fortunately, math has always been easy for me, so this didn't present too much of a problem.

Just to make things interesting during the thirteen-hour flight, I bet with some of the crew that we would arrive within twenty miles and five minutes of my projections. Fyrtle Myrtle landed three miles and one minute off, which added to my Hawaiian entertainment kitty, as well as adding a helluva lot to my self-confidence, but it did make it a little harder to find people to bet with after that.

When I walked into the operations room at Hickam, I saw my name on a sign on the bulletin board, saying that I was to call Colonel W.C. Farnum at Headquarters immediately. Louise, his wife, had written

Cush that I would be passing through in the spring on my way to Australia. Cush was now the Commanding Officer (CO) at Hickham Field. His Ford bore a battle scar from December 7 when it was parked in the driveway of his home near Pearl Harbor. He had a very close call that morning when he ran outside to see what all the commotion was about. Just as he got to the car, Louise screamed "Cush! Get back here! NOW!!" Cush, who was used to issuing orders rather than following them, heard something in the urgent tone of Louise's voice that told him not to question that order. He was no sooner in the door when a hail of bullets from a Japanese fighter strafed the lawn where he had been standing and left a hole in the Ford's left rear fender. Dependents were ordered to leave the Islands ASAP. Louise phoned my mother, who invited her and their nine-year-old son, Bill, to stay with her and my father until they could find a place of their own to wait it out.

Following the orders so conspicuously posted in the Operations room, I called Cush and he came right over. He said to tell my crew that I was going to be his guest, and to leave his phone number with them in case of sudden orders to leave. When we reached his quarters, I started to change into pajamas—we'd been flying all night and I was tired.

"Bill, what the hell're you doing?" Cush demanded, "We're going to a party!"

Since an order from a superior must be carried out, I got dressed again. There were some pretty Chinese girls at the party, but newly married to Betty, I had no incentive to get too friendly.

Pearl Harbor remained Headquarters of the U.S. Pacific Fleet and its Commander was Admiral Chester W. Nimitz. As CO of a major air facility, Cush had constant business with the Fleet Commander's staff. One evening he was invited to a party with top brass and took me along. As I remember, there were about forty guests, mostly Admirals and Generals—no one below the rank of Major except Second Lieutenant me. Believe me, I did a lot of "Yes, Siring" and "Yes, Maaming." My ever-gracious mother sent a note to Cush to pass along to Admiral Nimitz that elicited the following reply. (see opposite page)

July 13 1943

Dear Mrs. McFerren:

Colonel Farnum has just this moment left my headquarters after presenting me with your note of June 28, which I greatly appreciate. I particularly hope that I may be able to live up to the high expectations of your son and yourself.

It was a great pleasure to meet your son, and I repeat again that I hope to have the pleasure of pinning a medal on him under conditions and surroundings similar to those of the ceremony he witnessed at Hickam Field.

The information which you have just given me of the four prospective fathers in the crew of the "Fyrtle Myrtle" will henceforth command my special interest in that gallant ship's future.

Be assured that every officer and enlisted man of all the services in the Pacific is united in the determination to bring this war to an early and successful conclusion. With the support of men and women like yourself we can not fail!

With kindest regards and best wishes.

Sincerely yours,

C. W. Nimitz

C. W. NIMITZ

Mrs. Marjorie Welles McFerren,
502 East Penn Street,
Hoopeston, Illinois.

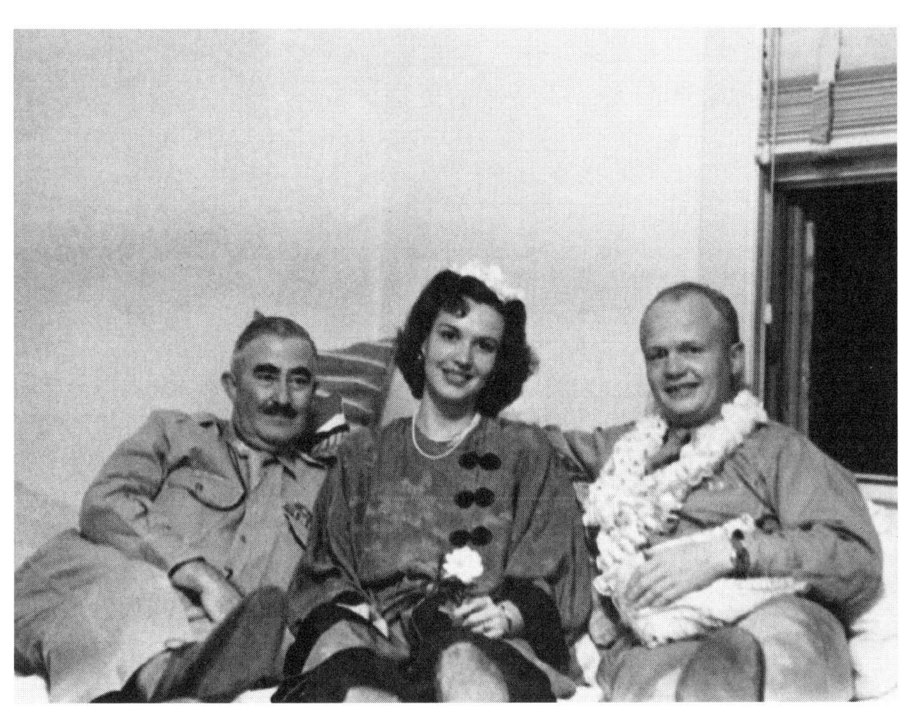

Colonel Cush Farnum, Ruth Dillingham, Lt. Bill McFerren
Hawaii, May 5, 1943

During our five days in Hawaii, I played a lot of bridge and poker. In one hand of five-card stud, I had a pair of deuces showing. Another player had a jack, queen, and king showing. Any one of them paired would beat me, but he made a psychological mistake. He bet the whole pot, which was $750. That suggested to me that he just didn't want me to stay. If he had wanted to sucker me along, he might have bet a couple of hundred tops, so I called and he didn't have a damn thing! My pair of deuces was high!

Hawaii was a wonderful civilized interlude before island hopping to the Australian outback. Our first stop was Canton Island, a small atoll about 1,700 miles southwest of the Hawaiian Islands, with a crushed coral airstrip marked by two palm trees. Al Paris reminded me after the war that it was the only airstrip he'd ever landed on that had a curve in it—the island simply wasn't big enough for it to run straight or it would have ended in the sea! Facilities there were built only as an airman's bed and breakfast en route to the Southwest Pacific. About a month earlier, the famous race car driver, Eddie Rickenbacker missed the atoll and had to ditch at sea. He drifted in a life raft for forty days before being found, luckily still alive but sunburned. He was rescued by a PBY Flying Boat. Not to be outdone by Rickenbacker, one of the 380th also missed it.

As a duty station, Canton Island was about as remote as they come. The local gag was that there had been one woman on the island. She died a month ago and they haven't buried her yet! Pretty raunchy but you get the idea.

A sergeant offered me $75 for a bottle of booze. I told him that I'd let him have one bottle at my cost if he'd personally see to it that Fyrtle Myrtle was carefully serviced. He was delighted and our airplane got lots of TLC. We then flew 1,300 miles to Fiji, and 800 miles to New Caledonia, resting overnight at each stop.

MacArthur, after being chased out of the Philippines, had set up headquarters at Brisbane, about midway up Australia's East coast. Under General George C. Kenney, the Fifth Air Force, of which we were a part, answered to General MacArthur, but our orders came from the

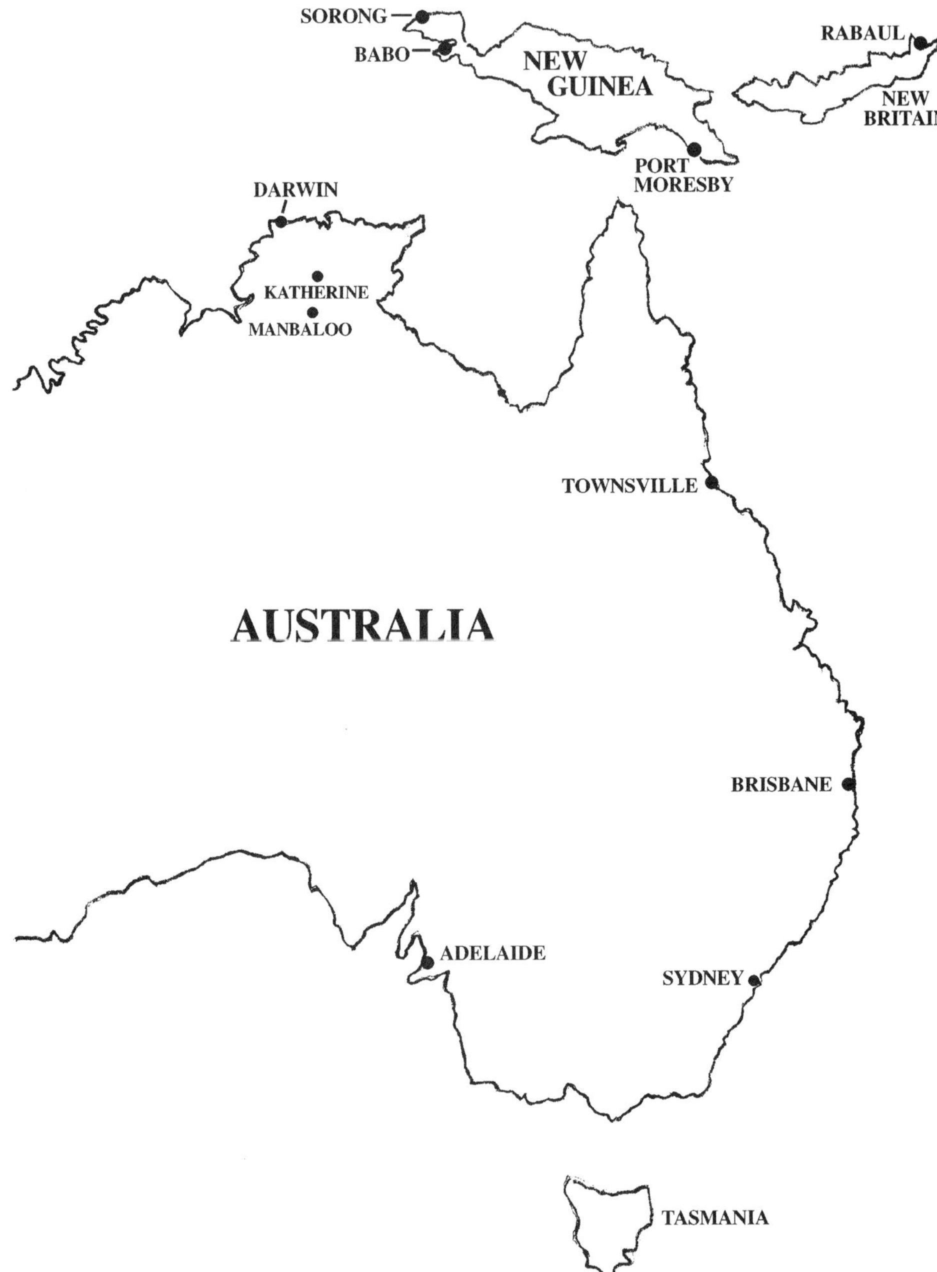
SORONG
BABO
NEW GUINEA
RABAUL
NEW BRITAIN
PORT MORESBY
DARWIN
KATHERINE
MANBALOO
TOWNSVILLE
AUSTRALIA
BRISBANE
ADELAIDE
SYDNEY
TASMANIA

RAAF Catalina Flying boat down off the Celebes.
Located and photographed by 380h B-24.
Photo #1 shows crew waving, sea anchor out.
Photo #2 shows rescue Catalina anchored alongside.
Photo #3 shows transferring crew in rubber raft.
Photo #4 shows downed plane straffed to prevent it falling into enemy hands.

RAAF (Royal Australian Air Force), which also answered to General Kenney (if that makes any sense to you. It didn't to us either). So be it not ours to reason where or why—what did make sense to us was, now that we were pseudo Aussies, we received two 24-ounce bottles of strong beer weekly, which seemed to be the birthright of every British or pseudo-British officer. Just one of them was enough to either (1) make me forget how lonely I was for Betty or (2) exacerbate my loneliness to such depths that I could practically taste it.

Once in Australia, Myrtle got a face-lift. Her "greenhouse" nose provided excellent vision but no protection whatsoever for the bombardier and nose gunner. Her pregnant guppy profile changed a bit when her plexiglass nose was replaced by an armored gun turret. After these modifications, Myrtle then carried a total of ten 50-caliber machine guns—two in the nose, two in the top turret over the wings, two on each side of the waist, and two in the tail.

A 50-caliber bullet (or round, as it is termed militarily) is a formidable projectile, half an inch across and weighing almost two ounces. It travels about 3,000 feet per second and could easily disable the engine of a pickup truck. Twin 50s fired about 300 rounds per minute. Flying in tight formation, a B-24 squadron (9 planes) presented enormous firepower against attacking fighters.

The site of this retrofit was Townsville, 300 miles north of Brisbane. When referring to a town of any size in Australia, it is hardly necessary to mention that it is on the seacoast. They are all on the seacoast. The inland or "outback" is pretty much desert.

Alterations took about two weeks, then it was on to our ultimate destination, Fenton Field, a 5,000-foot gravel strip in the outback about 100 miles south-southeast of Darwin, the major seaport at the northernmost tip of Australia's Northwest Territory. This is where our work began in earnest; I mean "grunt" work not at all directly related to flying.

CHAPTER 6

PLAYTIME IN TOWNSVILLE

Fenton Field, our home for the foreseeable future was a letdown to say the least. I had envisioned an installation somewhat like the other fields we had known, complete with Officer's Club, Operations room, etc. Even the words—Fenton Field—had an established, military ring to them. Such a concept was like our pioneers thinking they were going to put up their oxen and wagons at a Holiday Inn. As it turned out, it was up to us to build the Holiday Inn. The Corps of Engineers had done their part by bulldozing out a fairly level landing strip and erecting a few flimsy shacks for mess halls, maintenance, etc. Bathing was accomplished by lugging a five-gallon can of water to a convenient tree, hanging it up, and attaching a hose. Privacy? There wasn't any.

Living accommodations consisted of a wooden floor and frame, which we built (naturally), covered by a tent. Our crew drew the short straw and was assigned to dig a 10x10x10-foot garbage pit. After several unsuccessful attempts to drive a shovel into the rock hard ground, exasperated I thought, "There has to be an easier way." Suddenly it dawned on me that I had heard blasting in the distance where crews were dynamiting out a road and the idea light went on. I asked John Farrington, who didn't smoke, if he had any cigarettes from his ration that he didn't need. John's agile mind caught on quickly when I told him I needed some to dig a garbage pit with, and he gave me a carton.

Cigarettes, like booze, had become a medium of exchange. Four packs of cigarettes would get you six steaks and two pounds of butter from local farmers. However, as more of our people arrived with cigarettes, inflation set in and prices went up, but it was still a good deal

Crocodile Country:

(Left to right):
Dan Glendon,
James DeGroat,
Howard Sleighter,
Lou Glavin,
James Lovett,

(Standing):
James Lovett,
John Lardin,
(In the water):
James DeGroat,
Lou Glavin,
Dan Glendon

The crew goes hunting.

Outback barber

Staff Sgt. Dan Glendon foxhole digging.

Ant hill

Home, Sweet Home

from our point of view. Cigarettes in hand, I borrowed a jeep and set off in search of the road gang. I located the engineer in charge and told him my sad story, adding, "By the way, I've got a carton of cigarettes." He immediately pricked up his ears and agreed not only to give me the dynamite but the expertise to use it as well. We drilled a hole about five feet deep, packed it with dynamite, pushed a cap in the top, lit the fuse, and ran like hell. Instead of the anticipated pit, there was a very small dent in that hard-packed, bone-dry earth.

Back to the bartering table. I collected two more cartons of smokes and headed for the road gang again. This time success was ours and the result looked more like a garbage pit, but, hearing the explosion, Colonel Miller figured we were being bombed and came rushing over. He took one look and screamed, "McFerren, just what the hell do you think you're doing?"

"The medics said we needed a garbage pit, Sir. We just dug it," I replied.

"I'll be a son of a bitch," was all he could think of to say, then turned and walked away.

When ordinance personnel joined the Group, they did any further excavation needed via "leakers," which were bombs that had been left out in the sun too long and were starting to ooze. No one would intentionally load a leaker on a plane, and if by chance one did get loaded, we were instructed never to bring it back.

Not long after we arrived at Fenton, Japanese reconnaissance made a note of it and sent a welcoming committee to bomb us. Not too much damage was done by the Japs' two-motored "Betty" bombers, but we started digging slit trenches like our lives depended on it. A slit trench is about five feet deep and runs in a zigzag pattern so you have protection no matter from what direction the attack comes. It was a helluva lot of work but the Japs provided plenty of incentive.

Fortunately we didn't have to use our trenches because the enemy wasn't very good at night raids, and Aussie Spitfires, now alerted, provided effective daytime interception.

Major Fred Miller did his best to discipline some sort of maturity and physical fitness into a bunch of mischievous kids, and thank God he did because it probably saved some lives. He put all the officers in the squadron (or what was left of them) through calisthenics several mornings a week. One day as the Group was doing jumping jacks, he was astonished to see me sitting on a folding chair. He came charging over and bellowed "McFerren, just what in hell is going on here?"

Billy Massy, our bombardier, interrupted the Major with his soothing Alabama drawl. "Now just a minute, Major, Sir," Billy said in a manner that couldn't possibly irritate a flea, "You know we're flying over some pretty desolate territory, and if we should be forced down, we're going to need something good to eat. Porky here—I've been feeding him the best food—the finest steaks, pork chops, with biscuits and gravy. I'm trying to fatten him up so we can eat him. Now it just wouldn't be right to have him do a lot of exercise and work off all that good meat, would it?" Billy always had such a sweet smile and such a kind expression in those blue eyes of his. The Major grunted, scratched his head and mumbled, "I give up." The upshot—I was "Porky" from that day henceforth.

Charlotte, Billy and Bill Massey

One idle mind in our Group discovered that a razor blade crammed in the neck of an empty beer bottle and tossed from a plane made a shrill screaming noise like a falling bomb. Proof was the way the natives would scatter when we dropped those pseudo bombs near their New Guinea villages. Unfortunately during one such prank, a bottle made a hole in one of the vertical stabilizers in Myrtle's tail. This mishap plus some necessary adjustments in the new nose turret sent us back to Townsville for two weeks' worth of repairs.

We perceived this to be a rare opportunity to replenish liquor supplies. Word quickly got around and before I knew it, I had orders for about $10,000 Aussie dollars worth of booze. ($3.28 Aussie dollars equaled $1.00 US.) When we arrived in Townsville, I contacted a wholesaler who assured me he could take care of us, probably assuming we were talking about two or three cases. When I laid all that money out on the desk, he damn near died. All told, the order amounted to 40 cases of rum, 30 cases of vodka, 10 cases of scotch (we had orders for more but that was all they had), and 10 cases of bourbon. Then we hit a snag—it was a bonded warehouse and liquor couldn't be sold legally for consumption within the country to anyone without a dealer's license. I thought quickly and said that we were taking it to our base in New Guinea. The Aussies were always most cooperative, so he didn't ask further questions and made out the necessary papers. After a homeward flight of about an hour, John set Myrtle down as gently as if he were landing on eggs. Needless to say, we arrived to a tumultuous welcome.

An amusing incident occurred when some of the boys stole a very handsome fighting cock from a certain locale as a mascot. They decided to take him along on a mission for luck, but to their dismay, they found that despite the fact he had been very well behaved previously, flying made him nervous, and you know what a chicken does when he's nervous! He first flew up on the pilot's shoulder, left his mark, then onto the copilot, then all over the dashboard. His next direct hit was on the radio operator's head. They finally put him up in the top turret, but when the gunner took his seat in that position, he received a sad surprise. Needless to say, that was Jake's last mission. To add to his popularity, Jake then proceeded to get everyone up the next morning about 5 A.M. Are you beginning to see why our bunch got the "Flying Circus" moniker?

Jim Fain from Group Headquarters in his book, *The Flying Circus*, explains it better than I can, so thanks to Jim, I'll just include an excerpt from his book:

> "How did the 380th come to be called the Flying Circus, anyway?"
> The questioner was a crew member just assigned to the group, sitting in a tent on Okinawa soon after V.J. Day.
> "Oh, that goes way back to Lowry Field," another member of the squadron answered him. "It was like this. . .
> "General Eubank (Brig. Gen. Eugene I. Eubank, Air Corps Director of Bombardment and former commanding officer of the famed 19th Bomb Group) was pulling an inspection of our outfit.
> "Some of the brass in the group decided to meet him with a guard of honor, ignoring the fact that most of the Air Corps personnel in the group had never had basic training and knew nothing of drill. Still the guard was formed, equipped with rifles, and put into something looking like a formation down on the hangar line.
> "When the general dismounted, he saw the guard and thought it would be a good idea to inspect it. 'Open them up, and I'll come through,"' he told the non-com in charge, who luckily or unluckily, knew what that meant and gave the order: 'Prepare for inspection...open ranks...and march.'
> "The guard was baffled by the order but used their own judgment on the command 'open ranks' and scattered from hell to breakfast.
> "A few similar experiences, and General Eubank was heard to remark, 'My God, it's a flying circus.' "

During our stay in Townsville, I met the skipper of an LST (American Landing Ship Tank), who formerly taught at Vermont University. He was the father of three, but told me the old story that his wife didn't understand him. He had met an 18-year-old native girl who did understand him and was carrying on a torrid affair. He told me that after the war he intended to come back and live with her. (He didn't mention any more about the three kids.) However his love for the 18-year-old didn't keep him from asking "Do you know any girls here in town?"

I told him "Sure, there are a lot of nice Australian WACs,"

He started counting, "Let's see, there're four officers from your crew and five from mine, so we'll need nine girls plus one for me." I got in touch with the WAC I knew and she rounded up nine more. I promoted the booze and the steaks and a good time was had by all. Some of us got a little too much to drink including our pilot, John, who, unfortunately, was the soberest one, so we elected him to drive the truck home. He promptly ran it into a ditch. In those times, it seemed almost mandatory to have as much crazy fun as we possibly could before returning to the grizzly business at hand and the uncertainty that comes from getting shot at.

One night at the O Club, I ran into one of my former classmates at Yale. Of course I asked what he was doing there.

"I'm in command of a sub chaser, "he said, "and we're in for repairs. Things are terrible. We get our ass shot off every time we leave the harbor. We don't have enough armor."

I asked why he couldn't get the needed armament.

"I have to have a requisition and they won't give me one."

"What about Perth on the other coast?" I asked.

"I've tried that but we have to have a bloody requisition there too," he told me. (We were beginning to speak like Aussies.) In the course of the discussion, he mentioned that he had twenty cases of Johnny Walker Black Label on board. I asked, "If you could get the armor you need, how many cases would you be willing to spare?"

He did some mental arithmetic, "Oh, about fifteen,"

I told him "That may just be your requisition."

We loaded the whiskey in a jeep and headed for the field to call on the engineering officer. I introduced myself and said, "I have a friend here who has a sub chaser that's getting the hell shot out of it every trip. He needs some additional armament."

He replied with the standard, "He needs a requisition" line. "By the way," I added, "he just happens to have an extra fifteen cases of Johnny Walker Black Label."

The officer grinned and said, "By George, that sounds like a requisition to me." He got on the phone and in no time there was a small army of men ready, willing, and able to do the job. In a few days they had installed enough 50-caliber machine guns and three-inch cannon so that sub chaser looked like a miniature battleship. Those fifteen cases of scotch may well have saved a lot of Allied lives.

Unfortunately not all the fun ended upbeat. Freddy Miller had been on extended duty in New Guinea, and upon returning, joined us in Townsville to unwind. At the airfield where we bunked, there were four identical barracks surrounding the showers and latrine. It was hard to get rooms there but Freddy was lucky enough to do so. This also gave him access to the O club. Festivities had gone on a bit too long one evening, and Freddie stumbled out of the central washroom and ended up in the wrong barracks. When he got to what he thought was his room, the key wouldn't fit. Enraged, he banged on the door, yelling some unprintable words.

A voice inside growled "Beat it. This is my room,"

More verbal exchange, growing louder and angrier. "Bullshit, get out of here!" from within. Freddie took a run at the door and knocked it off its hinges. He grabbed the Captain within and threw him out the window. The next thing Freddie knew four MPs unceremoniously tossed him in the jug. It began to look as though our Squadron Commander would get court-martialed and possibly kicked out of the Air Corps. The only thing that saved him was that one member of the hearing board had been a good buddy of his in flight school. The upshot was that Major Miller got off with a $600 fine, big money in those days, but he was lucky and kept his commission.

In 1942 and early 1943, the war in the pacific continued going against the Allies. The enemy kept taking island after island and fortifying them well for expected counterattacks. Heroic naval battles—the four-day Battle of the Coral Sea in May 1942 followed by the decisive but horrendously costly Battle of Midway in June (in which all four Japanese carriers were sunk and the U.S. lost its carrier Yorktown)—slowed the enemy advance, but Japan still controlled the Dutch East Indies and everything north, including Malaysia, Singapore, and most of New Guinea. MacArthur and the Pacific Command were apprehensive that a Japanese invasion of the Australian continent was imminent. The Aussies were short on defense because almost all of their regular troops were already halfway around the world fighting in support of the British in North Africa. *(See excerpts from Jack Field's book, Rendezvous With Destiny, in Appendix.)*

Our Pacific Command was miffed that Washington allocated most military resources to the war in Europe, even though it was actually the Japanese that forced the United States to enter the war. Facing this 'beat Germany first' policy, MacArthur had to beg for ships and planes just to keep the Japanese in check. Deployment of the 380th Bomb Group to the Pacific instead of Europe was one of Washington's crumbs thrown to this critical situation.

The prime purpose of the 380th was to conduct armed recces (reconnaissance missions) and attacks on the threat to MacArthur's exposed western flank. Based on information so obtained, orders were to bomb airfields, oil and mining facilities, and shipping in the Dutch East Indies, all vital to the enemy war effort. Our job was to harass them, forcing them to use their resources to defend those areas lying beyond their extended lines, thus delaying any massing of forces for an assault on the Port Moresby area of New Guinea or Australia itself. This strategy must have worked because we got more bang for the buck than our thin resources gave us the right to expect.

Censorship did not allow me to tell Betty any of the preceding in my letters, as all correspondence was subject to military censorship. Those in charge of screening out anything that could be termed 'classified' would slit one end of the envelope, scan its contents, cut or black out any forbidden subject matter and tape the envelope closed. Anything to do with locations, operations, missions, repairs, and command structure—in fact anything remotely military—was verboten, which made my letters very vague and pretty dull. Thus, I had to invent ways to communicate what was going on. In one letter I told her, "I missed writing yesterday as I took your friend Myrtle to the ball game. She is a very amusing girl and I'm glad you told me to look her up. We had a swell time although the other team wasn't very good."

For me the arrival of mail was an even better morale booster than booze. It was the balm that helped to sooth the deep ache of separation and to maintain a link with the saner world of home and family. There were long periods of no mail when we were away from base. During those times it was particularly hard to cope with the stress of our business. Sometimes it took three or four weeks for a letter to arrive from the states; other times mail went much faster. It could pile up at distribution centers and then come in bunches, but Betty and I accepted those little inequities and were just grateful for any mail service at all.

CHAPTER 7

ODE TO A FLYING BOXCAR

I have logged about 500 combat and noncombat hours as navigator in Consolidated Aircraft's B-24 Liberator, most of that time aboard Fyrtle Myrtle. She was a collection of 1,250,000-nuts and bolts, several miles of control cable and a million other parts, powered by four 1,250 horsepower Pratt and Whitney engines that carried her crew faithfully over almost 41,800 miles of shark infested water, steamy jungles, and armed enemy installations.

Depending on who you talk to, the B-24 was either a dream or a nightmare to fly. Myrtle's pilot, John Farrington, affectionately known as "Mother," would never knock the plane—she was our ticket to life. When I visited with Al Paris after the war, he was more pragmatic. He said it was a tough airplane to keep in trim. I have always felt sure that if Al had been in the right-hand seat on that last mission, he would never have allowed us to linger over the target (waiting for a hot-shot pilot who wouldn't get back in formation) long enough for fighters a hundred miles away at Kendari to scramble and intercept us. But, as the saying goes, that's another story.

B-24s hold many records that were never broken. More of them were built, beginning in 1939 when the first B-24 rolled off the assembly line, than any other aircraft of the time, military or civilian—18,479 of them to be exact. They flew more missions and dropped more bombs than any other airplane.

Qualifications? 300 miles per hour top, better than 3,000-mile range, able to reach 30,000 feet altitude, all unequaled until late in the war when B-29 super-fortresses came on line. B-24s served in every theater of war flying under flags of fifteen different nations. In short, it was a workhorse. Its still unmatched record is testimony not only to

The 529th Squadron maintenance section atop Ready Teddy, a member of the elite 100 mission club.

NO KIDDING

The B-24 WWII bomber:

Heat in plane:
none

Temperature:
reached 40 - 50 degrees below zero

Room to stretch:
virtually none

Bathrooms:
none (flights lasted 8-10 hours.

Plane's aluminum skin:
cuttable by knife

Windshield wipers:
none

(courtesy American Heritage Magazine)

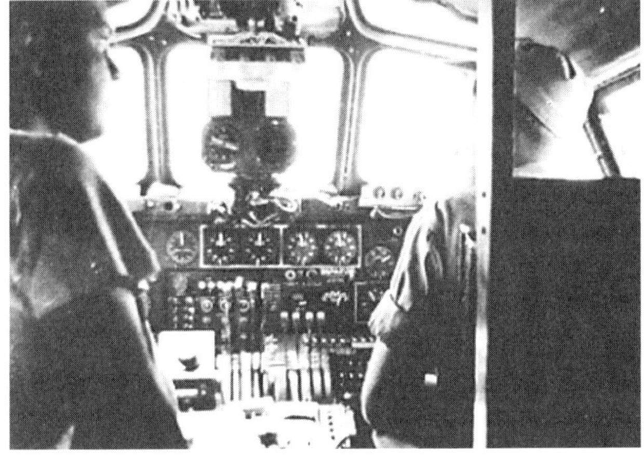

Pilot John Porter tends to his 'office'.

528th formation over Darwin.

Patty's Pig returned to Darwin, her two left engines out.

Captain Cliff Toepperwein's *Lady Jeanne II* with most of her controls disabled and only one good engine, crash lands close to home. One broken leg but no one killed.

the brave crews that flew them, but to the dedicated ground crews that kept them dependably in the air. Whether this awesome 18 by 66-foot monster returned intact from a milk run, or shot full of holes with leaky oil lines and instruments out of kilter, ground crews had it repaired and ready to fly as fast as humanly possible. Those guys were great and I don't think they ever got enough credit for the tedious hours they spent making sure that if we did run into trouble, it wouldn't be from mechanical failure.

Fifty-six holes were counted in the hide of "Beautiful Beast" when she limped home from one mission.

Just how did B-24s come to be? Back in aviation's 'dark ages' in the 1920s and early 1930s, the Army didn't see much necessity for long-range bombers, believing such contraptions were an offensive weapon that would never be needed. Makes you think of a common belief in the early 1900s –'the automobile was just a passing fancy and not here to stay.' A joke of that era told of an early day motorist who stopped at a farm to get water. Asked by the farmer what was that noisy contraption, the driver replied that it was an 'automobile.' "Wal," said the farmer pointing to a big rusty machine, "That's an oughta mow hay, but it don't."

By 1934, however, more far-sighted individuals clamored so loudly that ideas began to change and the B-17 showed up on drawing boards, able to deliver a three-ton bomb load with a range of about 2,880 miles. Soon though, the Army realized that might not be enough—distances in the Pacific were greater. Designers came up with the B-24 Liberator which was like a swan, ungainly and lumbering on the ground but in its natural habitat in the air, graceful and majestic. Its appearance on the ground earned it the nickname Flying Boxcar along with some other uncomplimentary and unprintable ones. The efficient but fragile "Davis' wing was placed high on the fuselage. Tanks held 2,500 gallons of high-octane fuel, with an extra 500 gallons possible in bomb-bay tanks. The cavernous interior could serve as a cargo or personnel transport in addition to its primary role as a messenger of death and destruction when fully loaded with five tons of high explosives.

Early Liberators cost $375,000 a copy before December 7, 1941. A few were sold to Britain for use in Ferry Command and reconnaissance. Australia bought a few—just in case.

After Pearl Harbor, Consolidated Aircraft, Ford Motors, and other manufacturers halted all civilian production and converted swiftly to supplying military needs. Using mass production methods, the price of B-24s came down to around $215,000. Ford built a plant at Willow Run that turned out Liberators by the thousands, of which Myrtle was one.

To me, it is mind boggling to realize that with the United States so woefully unsuspecting and unprepared on December 7, 1941, plus a devastating loss of men and materiel, the country was able to tool up, and by dint of sheer determination, skilled labor and engineers working around the clock, plus a singleness of purpose by every American citizen, was able to produce a war machine capable of winning that far-flung war in less than four years! The price in dollars was immense and the cost in lives infinitely worse, but it had to be done. Frankly it's food for thought to speculate as Herman Wouk does in *Winds of War*—what might have been the outcome if the U.S. had not been forced into war? Both England and Russia had been at war with the Nazi war machine for two years and their chances were looking pretty dismal at that point.

It has been said that if there were an endangered species of aircraft, B-24s would head the list. There are only two that I know of restored to mint condition and flying today—Diamond Lil of the Confederate Air Force and All American owned by the Collings Foundation of Stowe, Massachusetts. What an indescribable thrill it was a few years back at a Confederate Air Force show in Harlingen, Texas, to see Diamond Lil come thundering across in front of the grandstand barely twenty feet off the ground. Al Paris was invited to come to Harlingen to fly the B-24.

All American was restored by private contribution and thousands of man hours volunteered by nearly 2,400 devoted individuals. She appears at more than 100 events a year and costs around $2,000 an hour to fly, but those that love and respect this backbone of the Pacific War are not about to let it become only a memory. The prophetic words of

George Hilton, Professor Emeritus of Economics at UCLA, in his foreword to my brother-in-law Stan Garvey's book, *King and Queen of the River* (the true story of twin riverboats built only twelve years before the first Liberator took to the air), apply to All American and Diamond Lil just as surely as they do to historic steamers: "It would be hasty to conclude that the old steamers will survive indefinitely... It is not in the nature of ships of any sort to go on forever. We would be well-advised to experience both these steamboats while we can."

The plane was designed to have a gross weight, including bombs, fuel, and crew, of about 58,000 pounds max. We often pushed that to around 65,000 or more for extended missions, such as the ones to Balikpapan, Borneo.

Liberators were far from luxurious—no creature comforts, period. We brown bagged our meals and carried a thermos of coffee. The cabin wasn't pressurized, had no kitchen or restroom, and minimal heating. There was oxygen for use above 10,000 feet, but we seldom flew higher than that because it was too costly in fuel. Fortunately Japanese ack ack couldn't go nearly as high as German AA.

For ditching at sea there were two deflated life rafts stowed on top of the fuselage. (I owe my life to one of them.) To bail out, there were seven emergency exits—you could depart from the nosewheel well, the astrodome, a top hatch, the bomb bay, either waist gun position, or down through the main hatch just forward of the tail. The main thing was to remember to wait at least three seconds to pull the ripcord till you were well away from the plane.

Liberators served in every theater of war. They flew low-level raids on the Romanian oil fields at Polesti where hundreds were lost, but those suicidal missions neutralized twenty-five percent of the Axis vital oil supply. The debate over B-24s versus B-17s will go on as long as the men live who flew them. Consensus was that the 17 was a more forgiving plane to fly and could return home after more brutal punishment, such as having chunks of rudder shot away and bullet holes everywhere—a quality that understandably endeared them to their crews. B-24s carried heavier loads over greater distance, but did require constant attention to keep in trim. This was an exacting task in formation and became a nightmare if you lost an engine.

Once they accepted these idiosyncrasies however, many crew members developed a growing affection for their plane. Its versatility allowed it to handle anything from high altitude bombing to treetop strafing and skip bombing (explained further in Chapter 9). After all we'd been through with Fyrtle Myrtle, the steady drone of her powerful motors a reassurance to our ears, I know that I felt a certain begrudging kinship for that faithful hunk of metal. Like it or not, she was all that stood between us and certain disaster.

After the war, some of these old war birds that were still alive were sold at fire sale prices for use as cargo transports or slurry bombers to fight forest fires. A number were bought by foreign airlines and retrofitted for passenger use and some became the property of private citizens. Over thirty years ago, with time to kill between connections at the old airport in Mazatlan, Mexico, I was thrilled to see a B-24 land and taxi down the concourse. Our combat aircraft used to have a scoreboard painted on the nose—a bomb for every mission, a plane for every fighter shot down. This civilian plane had a flag for every country it had visited, and it had many. It was owned by a wealthy Mexican who most courteously invited us aboard to see its plushy interior with soft leather couches and coffee tables, a compact kitchen and bar—very different from our flights into the wild blue yonder!

As if that weren't enough for one day, another antique landed – a Ford Tri-motor flew in from the mines in the State of Durango. Its original model was built in 1926, looked like it was made of corrugated steel, and was probably two or three times as old as its pilot. Tri-motors can take off and land on short runways at fairly high altitudes so are ideal for the mining country in the Durango mountains.

So there you have the curriculum vitae of Fyrtle Myrtle, who carried her crew 8,000 miles from the U.S. to Australia and on 18 1/2 missions throughout the South Pacific.

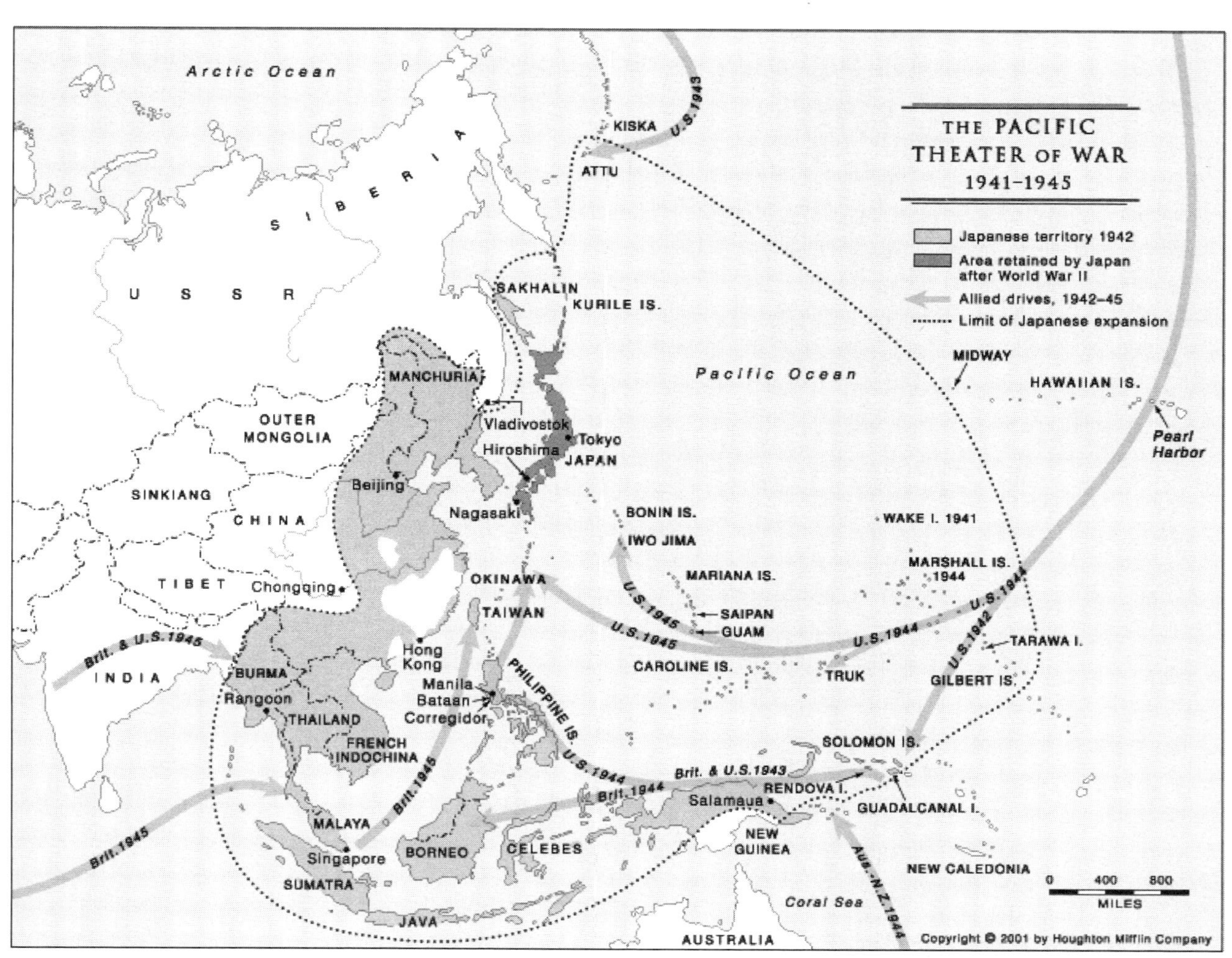
THE PACIFIC THEATER OF WAR 1941–1945
Japanese territory 1942
Area retained by Japan after World War II
Allied drives, 1942–45
Limit of Japanese expansion
Arctic Ocean
Pacific Ocean
Coral Sea
S I B E R I A
U S S R
OUTER MONGOLIA
SINKIANG
C H I N A
T I B E T
I N D I A
MANCHURIA
Beijing
Chongqing
Vladivostok
SAKHALIN
KURILE IS.
KISKA
ATTU
U.S. 1943
JAPAN
Tokyo
Hiroshima
Nagasaki
BONIN IS.
IWO JIMA
MIDWAY
HAWAIIAN IS.
Pearl Harbor
WAKE I. 1941
MARSHALL IS. 1944
MARIANA IS.
SAIPAN
GUAM
CAROLINE IS.
TRUK
TARAWA I.
GILBERT IS.
U.S. 1942
U.S. 1944
U.S. 1945
OKINAWA
TAIWAN
Hong Kong
Manila
Bataan
Corregidor
PHILIPPINE IS.
BURMA
Rangoon
THAILAND
FRENCH INDOCHINA
MALAYA
Singapore
SUMATRA
JAVA
BORNEO
CELEBES
NEW GUINEA
Salamaua
SOLOMON IS.
RENDOVA I.
GUADALCANAL I.
NEW CALEDONIA
AUSTRALIA
Brit. & U.S. 1945
Brit. 1945
Brit. 1944
Brit. & U.S. 1943
Aus.-N.Z. 1944
0 400 800 MILES
Copyright © 2001 by Houghton Mifflin Company

CHAPTER 8

COMBAT AT LAST

By July 1943, the tide finally began to turn against the Japanese. Our raids on their Dutch East Indies bases threw a monkey wrench in their continuing conquest in that area. They had thought those bases were beyond the range of Allied air attack, but our audacious long distance trips forced them to reconsider that assumption. As Allied strategic command hoped, the enemy was forced to divert personnel and materiel to defend vital supply routes that they previously considered safe. Little did they know that we were stretching everything to the limit, sometimes arriving home with only a few drops of gas left in our tanks—literally on a wing and a prayer. In fact, on Myrtle's last Balikpapan trip, the #2 and #4 engines sputtered and coughed as we reached the end of our runway—that's too close for comfort! But, I'm getting ahead of my story.

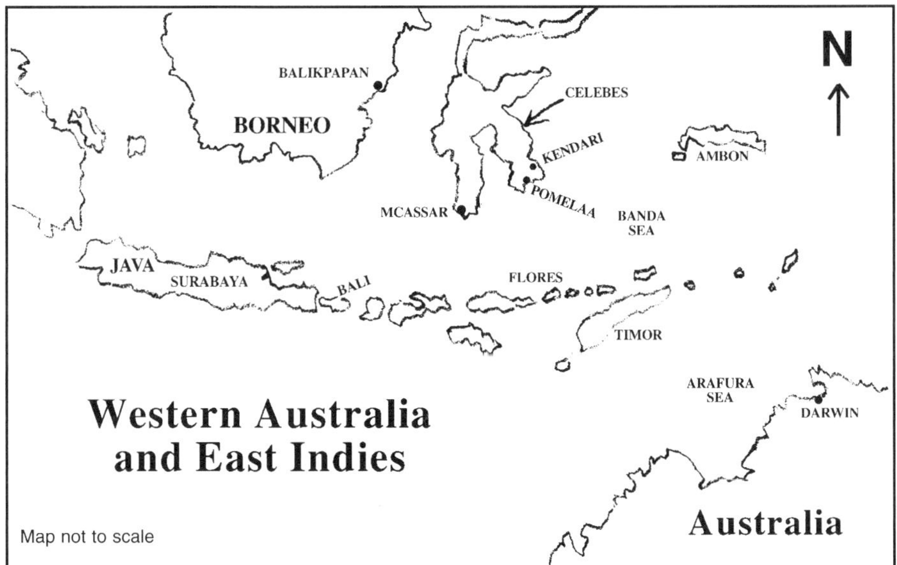

Vigilant Aussie Spitfires turned back most Jap attacks at Australia's north coast, which prevented them from learning our true strength, or lack of it. Had they known how thin we really were, they might have decimated us, as their supplies were so much closer than ours. Fortunately, we were winners in that strategic bluffing game. At least we didn't have to go to the lengths that Claire Chenault and his Flying Tigers out of China did in the days before Pearl Harbor when they were helping China fight the Japanese. They made early morning raids and returned home for lunch, then flew afternoon raids sometimes with a quick-dry paint job of a different color or design on the undersides of the wings, creating the impression that they had twice as many planes!

A careless mistake cost us a plane named Poochie coming home from a 'fat cat' trip to Sydney on the east coast to pickup fresh food, booze, and other essentials. Major Everett Ware, a West Point grad, was pilot and I was one of a couple dozen passengers. After loading up and preparing for the approximately 1,950 mile return trip, Billy Reese, navigator, advised Ware that we should take on extra fuel as onboard supplies were marginal. Ware disagreed, saying that we had plenty. He was the ranking officer so we took off. En route, an electrical problem shorted out the radio and the resulting confusion caused the crew to miss the fact that

Burned out Poochie

we had drifted off course. Even after being advised of this, Ware ignored corrections and when we reached the north coast, he didn't know whether we were east or west of Darwin. He had to admit that we were lost, very low on gas, and without a radio had no choice but to attempt an emergency landing. We didn't want to bail out because we hoped to save the supplies on board, not to mention the airplane.

Ware rejected a belly landing on the beach in favor of a wheels down landing on what looked like a smooth grassy area adjacent to the coast. As we touched down, we were horrified to see that the 'grass' was six feet high, dry and tough. The nosewheel collapsed immediately, and 25 tons of B-24, booze, and food stopped abruptly in about 100 yards. Bumps, bruises, and a possible broken ankle were the only human casualties, but Poochie was another story.

There was no water available so we decided the only thing to do was slake our thirst with sparkling Burgundy.

Fenton Field picked up our emergency beacon giving the rough whereabouts of their missing airplane. A recce mission was dispatched early the next morning to survey the problem. As it appeared on the horizon, one of our party, intending to be helpful but still charged up on sparkling wine, fired off some flares to pinpoint our location. The flares fell, still burning, into the tall dry grass upwind. We perceived immediately that Poochie was doomed and everyone started feverishly unloading her precious cargo before raging flames engulfed the taxpayers' $300,000 investment. Hungry and dirty, we arrived back at Fenton a couple of days later courtesy of some neighborly Aussies. Their reward for the rescue was most of the remaining booze. The buck stopped at the top and the hapless Major lost his job.

A B-17 pilot, Ed Carr, in his book, *On Final Approach*, tells a story from the other side of the world that is certainly worth repeating. Returning from Europe, his Flying Fortress was nearing a field in Newfoundland very low on gas. He was hoping for a break in the clouds to enable him to spot Meeks Field. Seeing a strip that he took to be the one he wanted, he was able to get the plane down safely, but realized it was not Meeks Field, as the runway was so short he had to use bare ground at its end to bring the plane to a halt. At least they were all in one piece. He radioed his bearings to the correct field, which was actually only a short distance away. A jeep was sent out to discuss the situation. The strip was too short to give them any chance of a successful takeoff. A decision was made to attempt an overland route since there was a dirt road and no underpasses. They radioed the field to be ready for what was probably the first arrival of a heavy bomber to drive in. Everyone cheered madly as the B-17, led by a jeep, emerged ghostlike from the mist, using its propellers not only for propulsion but for steering!

In spite of all the hi-jinks, Allied fortunes of war were slowly improving, but at terrible cost of lives and airplanes. In the first two months, the 531st Squadron had lost six crews and planes. This shocking statistic was not only due to enemy action but to inexperience, poor judgment, weather, carelessness, bad luck, etc. Group felt it necessary to shore up the 531st ranks by moving several crews from other squadrons.

Fyrtle Myrtle & Co. was assigned to the 531st Squadron in a rebuilding program. The only catch was that the 531st base was at Manbaloo, 80 miles southwest, so we were uprooted from our familiar abode and friends at Fenton and had to start over. One advantage though, a semblance of civilization—the tiny town of Katherine was

Although playful beach buzzing was not ordinarily cause for penalty, 1st Lt. Charles Boyle III was grounded for three months for scooping up sand on one low pass.

close and that meant available ice, eliminating the need for thirty-minute high-altitude 'training flights' to cool beer. We were located not far south of the equator, meaning that even though it was winter, temperatures often reached 90 to 100 degrees making ice more of a necessity than a luxury.

Our first combat mission was July 10—an 11-hour, 1,700-mile recce flight to Sorong on the extreme northwest tip of New Guinea. Orders were to survey that Japanese-held port and to attack any facility or ship we could find. There was no resistance from the ground, probably due to the element of surprise. Our second combat trip was a night mission to Makassar, a western seaport on the main Celebes island about 1,200 miles northwest of Manbaloo.

We couldn't fly there directly as that would mean passing over the island of Timor, held by the Japs. The flight plan involved giving Timor a wide berth, both going and coming. We returned frighteningly low on fuel. Thus we learned in the school of hard knocks about the effect detours or foul weather had on fuel consumption.

During one of our early missions, we were jumped by two Jap fighters. I learned the meaning of 'cool' from our stoical top turret gunner, Sgt. Louis Glavin. He came from North Dakota and as a kid shot quail on the wing with a 22 rifle. One of the tests in selection of gunners was ability on the skeet range. Training in El Paso, Louie's first effort broke 23 out of 25 and later he busted 25 even!

Japanese 'Tess' down at Pomelaa

When the first fighter came down from about 11 o'clock, it scared the hell out of me, but Glavin held his fire. I kept saying, "Louie, when are you gonna shoot?" and he just said "Relax,

Lieutenant," as he let loose a burst of tracers to get his range. The next burst nailed the Jap, and as the second fighter closed in, Louie had him in his sights and got him too.

Experience like that instilled confidence in one another that each person knew his job and would do it without cause for worry. Such early missions ensured a crew that worked harmoniously together under the stress of more combat to follow. Everyone had to stay constantly on guard because you never knew at what moment we might be fighting for our lives. Louie told me that shortly after arriving in Australia, he asked a seasoned old gunner how he knew when to shoot and what to shoot at. The answer was, "Son, we shoot at anything that ain't in the formation."

Another uneventful mission to Sorong wrapped up our July operations and life at Manbaloo settled into pretty much what it had been at Fenton, except for the advantage we now had ice. Actually we were on the edge of a tropical paradise, which under happier circumstances would have made us the envy of any pleasure-seeking tourist. Seas with exotic names like Coral, Banda, Timor, Flores, and Ceram have been aquatic highways for island people for millennia past. As seen from thousands of feet above, the shallow coral reefs and deep trenches presented a breathtaking mosaic of light and dark blue-greens. On many islands grew lush jungles inhabited by rare birds and plants, some of which may not even have been named yet by researchers.

The downside to all these tropical wonders was (1) we had a war to fight, though the antics described herein sometimes make one wonder how we ever won it, and (2) the hellaciously unpredictable weather, which was even more treacherous than the human enemy. The warm sea water (warmest in the world, somebody said) was responsible for ferocious thunderstorms that could make planned routes not only dangerous but at times, unworkable. Huge mushroom-shaped clouds are called cumulonimbus, and though they appear static, within them are powerful swirling winds that can literally twist a plane into a crumpled mass of junk.

Captain Jim Planck, in the 530th, went on to a career in the Air Force. He was quoted in the 'Yearbook," compiled by Gary and Glen, Horton, Jr., twin sons of Lt. Glenn Horton, "I've been flying for more than thirty years throughout the world in all kinds of weather, and can now say without hesitation the southwest Pacific weather conditions were the worst I have ever encountered. For six months out of each year, we flew through spine-chilling, bone-rattling, terror-ridden weather. Thunderstorms in these systems reached from the surface of the sea to altitudes up to 60,000 feet. They routinely spawned tornados, water spouts, torrential rains, hail, icing, and severe turbulence. It was difficult to imagine all the trouble one of these fronts could give you. I recall one particular mission that gave us quite a scare. We were headed north, moving toward a very dark, ominous horizon. As we drew closer, the strike leader called to the individual flights to make a 45 degree separation maneuver for safer weather penetration. Shortly after I turned our ship back on course, the dark clouds engulfed us. We were flying at 8,000 feet and had no sooner made our penetration when a strong updraft caught our heavily loaded bomber. We were being buffeted upward at an alarming rate in torrential rain. Water on the canopy could not have been any heavier if you had taken a fire hose to it. The noise was deafening amid brilliant lightening flashes. We continued our uncontrolled ascent past 20,000 feet, and the sky remained black as night. I think one of the most frightening realizations of the situation was that you had to fly through it again in order to get home. For those crews returning in battle-damaged airplanes, it must have been an immeasurably more harrowing experience. Personally, I will never forget it."

In downtime on scorching hot days, I used to take an air mattress down to a slow moving stream near the camp to relax and catch a few rays. Once while I was loafing around out there, someone shouted, "Porky, get the hell out of the water! There's an alligator after you!" I turned to see a salt-water crocodile coming my way. They are really dangerous. I paddled like hell for the shore and got there in time. We decided it was him or us, so we laid in wait for him with automatic

January 2004

Croc kills man in Australia, trees his 2 pals

By The Associated Press

DARWIN, Australia — A crocodile killed a 22-year-old man and then kept his body in its jaws while his two friends watched in horror from a nearby tree.

Shaun Blowers and Ashley McGough, both 19, recounted Tuesday how the reptile snatched Brett Mann at Finniss River, which cuts through a tropical wilderness southwest of Darwin in the Northern Territory on Sunday.

Blowers said the 13-foot saltwater crocodile also lunged at them, but they scrambled up a tree in the swollen stream. A police search party found them still in the tree 22 hours later.

The friends had been riding ATVs along a muddy trail, and stopped by the river to bathe.

Mann was swept away by a strong current. As his friends swam out to help, he was taken by a crocodile that had been lurking in the waters.

"We both jumped in and swam after him, and we got in front of him and were leading him back to the bank," Blowers said. "I went past the croc. I didn't see it. Ashley screamed out, 'Croc, croc!'... We just swam to the nearest tree and straight up we went.

"We were looking around for Brett (but) didn't hear a thing, didn't hear a scream, no splashing or anything," he said.

"Two minutes later the croc brought Brett to the surface and pretty much showed him off to us, and off he swam.

"Five minutes later he was back stalking the tree around us. He just hung around us all night and pretty much all the next morning."

A police helicopter took the survivors to Darwin, where they were treated for shock and exposure.

Authorities were searching the river for Mann's remains and for the man-eating crocodile.

Saltwater crocodiles are among the world's largest reptiles.

They became a protected species in 1971 after they were nearly wiped out over the past century. There are now an estimated 100,000 saltwater crocs, and there have been growing calls for a reintroduction of limited hunting.

Last year a crocodile killed a 25-year-old German woman as she swam in the Northern Territory.

rifles. Finally he crawled up on a sandbar and bang! bang! bang!, we let go about forty rounds. That ended any further sunbathing problems, at least with that croc, while also doing away with one crocodile hide for a number of fashionable shoes and women's purses.

In our spare time, we often supplemented the fresh food supply with fresh fish. Hooks and lines, etc. were in our survival kits, but some guys preferred to fish with explosives. This approach resulted in fabulous harvests, but was less than sporting in my piscatorial philosophy. It surprised me that we caught the same type of fish that I used to see back home in the Illinois streams—smallmouth bass and catfish. For bait we shot wallabies and used their livers to bait hooks. That may seem gross, but what the hell, it was wartime and humans were killing one another. Life was cheap and we needed irresistible bait.

Mail was becoming a real problem for the transport command. While wonderful for morale, its huge volume began to compete for space in transport planes with essential military supplies. A system called V-mail was devised whereby a one-page printed form for correspondence was reduced to microfilm, shipped by air, and at the receiving end, photocopied in enlarged form. The obvious advantage to this was its reduction in bulk and its speed in reaching the recipient, but the problem was that there wasn't much space for writing unless you used a typewriter, and if you typed it, then the finished product was reduced down so small that you almost needed a magnifying glass to read it. Oh, well.

CHAPTER 9

BUSINESS PICKS UP – BALIKPAPAN

Now that our long-range bombing had begun to accomplish its objectives by postponing Japanese plans to occupy all of New Guinea and points south, General MacArthur's number one priority was to take back the enemy-occupied part of New Guinea and also the Philippines. In preparation for that, he needed up-to-date information on all enemy movement in the entire Dutch East Indies.

Japan had to ship essential raw materials—oil, rubber, bauxite (used in manufacture of aluminum), tin and iron ore—across 2,700 miles of sea from the Indies north to Japan to keep its war machine supplied. Allied subs, surface ships, and carrier-based planes harassed their shipping lanes unmercifully. Our land-based bombers (the Flying Circus, among others) continued destroying their docks and airfields, which the Nips endeavored to rebuild as fast as we could dismantle them.

The Allies devised a clever trick called 'skipbombing,' which must have originated when someone skipped a flat stone across the surface of a pond. A two-engine Mitchell B-25 was first to try it. If conditions were right, skip bombing was the answer to the obvious difficulty of hitting a moving ship from high altitude because, unlike a warehouse or dock, a ship is not only a very small target but it can take evasive action, rendering the Norden bombsight useless (which some claim it was anyway). General Kenney refined the 'rock on the pond' technique by flying the bomber at top speed about 200 feet off the deck heading directly toward the target ship. About a quarter of a mile away, a 250-pound bomb is jettisoned and the plane pulls sharply up and away. Theoretically the bomb becomes something like a torpedo and penetrates the ship. A delayed-action fuse explodes it inside the hull. Gunners leave a goodbye message with their 50 calibers.

The B-25's skipbombing was so successful that General Kenney was anxious to give it a try with the longer range of a B-24. We practiced on a beached freighter off the coast of Darwin, This turned out to be great fun, and we did so well, we couldn't wait to try the real thing. Our first bona fide attempt was during rather poor visibility. We felt sure we had hit the freighter, but not seeing an explosion, thought we must have had a dud, then someone remembered the delayed-action fuse. Post-strike intelligence confirmed our success.

On August 13, we made the longest mission ever flown by heavy bombers at that time. Balikpapan on Borneo housed several major oil refineries that were as vital to the Japanese as the Polesti oil fields in Romania were to the Germans. Japan got at least half its lubricating oil and aviation gasoline there. This raid had to be planned and executed without any up-to-date intelligence information because making a recce trip would tip our hand. Surprise was paramount.

Primary orders were to do all possible damage to the refineries and to sink any ships in the harbor. It was important to leave no doubt in the Nip's mind that nothing was beyond the Allies' long reach.

About 6 P.M., twelve B-24s left Darwin for Balikpapan with an ETA (estimated time of arrival) after midnight. To aid vision, the raid was scheduled for a night of full moon. Not only did Darwin lie 100 miles closer to the target than Manbaloo, but it had a 10,000-foot runway. Our heavily loaded bombers needed every inch of those 10,000 feet to get airborne. We took advantage in every way we could to ensure success for that 2,700-mile trip. The Liberators were loaded to the gills with 3500 gallons of fuel and six 500 pound demolition bombs. The last few seconds before takeoff, with all four engines straining mightily, were pretty hairy—was 10,000 feet going to be enough? Fortunately, air is densest at sea level, and Myrtle was able to get off the ground. Her reliable Pratt and Whitneys defied gravity once more, and we settled back for a long and hopefully boring trip.

Weather interfered with that hoped-for boredom as we encountered several bad storms that caused two of the formation to abort, leaving ten aircraft to do the work. The plan called for half of us to skipbomb shipping at masthead level, while the others would make one or two conventional bomb runs around 7,000 feet.

We arrived over the target on schedule and it was lit up like a Christmas tree, but it didn't take the Nips long to figure out that they were under attack. They quickly doused the lights, but by then fire and explosions were keeping things illuminated. Anti-aircraft put a few holes in Myrtle's tail, but nothing too serious and our tail gunner, Jim Lovett, wasn't hurt. It was a highly successful mission and all planes retuned to Darwin very low on gas but intact and home safe and sound. It had been the equivalent of a flight from New York to San Francisco—sixteen hours in the air for a lumbering B-24.

At headquarters, Generals MacArthur and Kenney and the Australian Command were so jubilant over our long trip to Balikpapan that they awarded everybody two medals—the DFC and a Presidential Unit Citation.

Two days later, two planes went back to make a post-strike assessment. The wounds in Myrtle's tail took about a week to repair, then we bombed Balikpapan again just to make sure the Nips understood that the first strike wasn't a fluke like that incredible Billy Mitchell raid on Tokyo back in April 1942, when the U.S. was getting the you-know-what kicked out of it. That early day stunt led by Lieutenant Colonel James Doolittle was a gutsy effort to boost Allied standing and morale in those early dark days after Pearl Harbor. A flight of sixteen Mitchell B-25s took off from the carrier Hornet 600 miles off the coast of Japan, bombed Toyko, and flew on to any place they could find to land or crash in China. B-25s could not return to the Hornet—takeoffs were remarkable enough, but landings would be impossible! B-25s were not designed for carrier duty—no tail hooks or any other carrier qualifications.

Astonished Japanese heard radio broadcasts tell that the planes came from Shangri la. That daring fight was chronicled by the movie, "Thirty Seconds Over Tokyo," starring Van Johnson. The following San

Francisco Chronicle article dated May 15, 2002, tells a first-person account of that astounding raid less than five months after the attack on Pearl Harbor.

5/15/02

☆☆☆☆☆ San Francisco Chronicle A23

J. Royden Stork — B-25 bomber co-pilot in 1942 Doolittle Raid

By Myrna Oliver
LOS ANGELES TIMES

LOS ANGELES — J. Royden Stork, who as co-pilot of a B-25 bomber took part in a daring raid on Tokyo on April 18, 1942, and later went on to become a Hollywood makeup artist, died May 2 at Century City Hospital of a heart attack. He was 85.

The raid, led by Lt. Col. James H. Doolittle, was the first successful American retaliatory strike following Japan's bombing of Pearl Harbor, which brought the United States into World War II.

Mr. Stork was co-pilot of the 10th of 16 land-based B-25 bombers to take off from the deck of the aircraft carrier Hornet, a feat never before attempted and considered by many a suicide mission for the 80 men aboard.

Flying at treetop level, Mr. Stork's plane correctly bombed its assigned chemical plant and flew on until, like the others, it ran out of gas over occupied China.

"The 16 planes didn't do much damage, but we sure screwed up their war machine," Mr. Stork told the Boston Herald last month during 60th anniversary observances of the raid. "They had to pull back some of their forces to protect the (Japanese) homeland, and some of their military leaders were so humiliated that they committed suicide."

President Franklin D. Roosevelt orchestrated the raid, not for the limited bomb damage it could cause, but to boost sagging American morale and to shock the Japanese, who thought distance protected them from attack. Not only had the Japanese sunk most of the Pacific Fleet at Pearl Harbor, but in the intervening 132 days they had also defeated U.S. forces at Wake Island and in the Philippines.

Doolittle's raid made Americans believe they could win the war and step up their efforts to do it.

Not one of Doolittle's planes was lost to enemy fire. Of the 16, one crash-landed, three were ditched in coastal waters, one landed in Russia and the other 11 came down in China. Two of the 80 men drowned, and of eight captured, three were executed by Japanese, and one died in prison camp.

Mr. Stork was among a dozen or so of the fewer than two dozen members of the Doolittle Raiders Association still living who gathered last month in Columbia, S.C., for the group's 60th anniversary reunion.

He described his harrowing Doolittle Raid experience many times over the years, beginning with an article published by the Los Angeles Times shortly after the attack. Before parachuting out of the gasless plane, he said in that interview nearly six decades ago, he stuffed his pockets full of candy bars and cigarettes.

"Those bars were flung in every direction, my parachute gave me such a flip," he said. "It was pouring rain, and in no time my chute was soaked with water, and I was falling very fast. I couldn't see anything in the dark, so I was in a completely relaxed condition when I hit the ground. Otherwise I might have been hurt. I must have been knocked unconscious, as I don't remember anything until I found myself lying against a tree. I lay in the rain until morning before starting out."

The downed co-pilot walked for a day until he was befriended by a local Chinese magistrate who helped him get to the preassigned rendezvous point another three days away. Stationed afterward in India with the Army's 10th Air Force, Mr. Stork flew missions over Japanese occupied territory in the China-Burma-India theater for 16 months.

Mr. Stork was grounded from combat flying, along with the other 73 surviving Doolittle Raiders, when U.S. intelligence learned that the Japanese had put a $5,000 bounty on each of the fliers' heads.

Mr. Stork was born in Frost, Minn., grew up in San Diego and attended San Diego State University before joining the U.S. Army Air Corps on Nov. 25, 1940. He completed advanced flight training the following April, a year before he found himself aboard the Hornet with his destination unknown.

Last year, he was among veterans who attended the Honolulu premiere of the blockbuster movie "Pearl Harbor." He also was one of eight surviving Doolittle Raiders to meet with scriptwriter Randall Wallace to complain that both Doolittle and the raid were incorrectly depicted in the film.

Leaving Balikpapan. A later raid since our first two were nighttime.

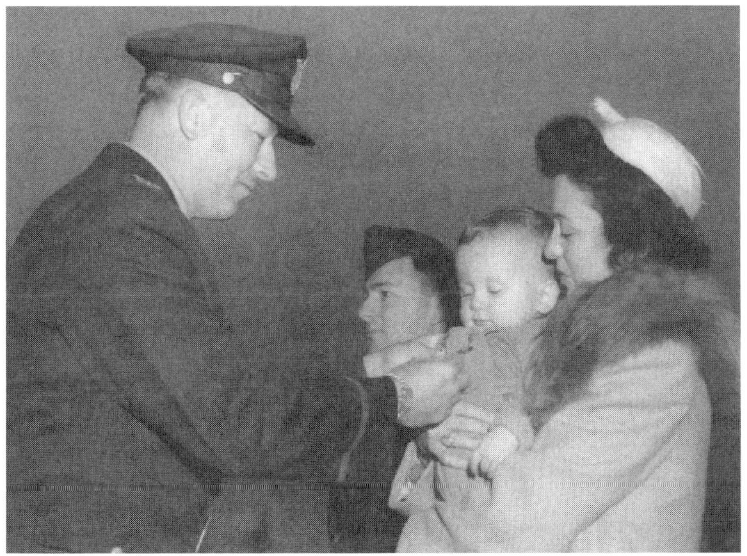

Young Bill receives his Daddy's DFC (Distinguished Flying Cross)
at March Field in recognition of the longest mission flown.
(The one to Balikpapan on August 13, 1943.)
His Daddy was missing in action at the time of presentation.

On our way to Balikpapan for our second raid, it was dark and we ran right into a monster tower of weather at about 3,000 feet. 72,000 pounds of plane and crew were being sucked upward about a mile a minute while our indicated forward speed showed we were doing only 90 miles an hour. A B-24 stalls out under normal conditions around 120 but this updraft was a lot stronger than aerodynamic principles. Myrtle's wings were flapping and cracking as though they might part company with the fuselage. More than one of us had wet pants or worse by the time we emerged on top at about 30,000 feet, but still in one piece. Everything suddenly became serene as I looked down at the hurricane beneath us. This dramatic switch to calm and quiet was surreal. Somehow we had managed to don our oxygen masks and get them connected while Myrtle was bucking like a wild bronco—at this altitude I was mighty glad I had mine on! I breathed a heartfelt thank you to Colonel Miller for his vigilance in Tucson for noting a flaw in the way the wings were attached to the fuselage, and insisting that it be corrected.

I heaved a sigh of relief, but we weren't out of the woods yet. A downdraft of equal intensity caught us (they can reach speeds of 100 miles an hour), and we started losing altitude at an alarming rate; the plane was again out of control and we were headed for the drink. John and Al must have used every trick in the books and a few that weren't just to keep the plane right side up. They dropped the landing gear and made a 20 percent adjustment in the flaps in an effort to gain some stability. I had no idea where we were but I knew we were running out of altitude fast, when just a few hundred feet off the water, the downdraft weakened and John and Al were able to gain control. We resumed our heading for Borneo where we were greeted with searchlights and ack ack, but thankfully no fighters, because it was nighttime.

As significant as those Balikpapan strikes were, the most satisfying one personally for me was later in August when we hit Babo, a big Zero (fighter) base in northwest New Guinea. In July we had lost three planes attacking that well-defended port and we wanted badly to destroy it. The big problem was a weather front that consistently hung over the area that time of year. Visibility wasn't good enough to allow us to fly tight formation in order to better defend ourselves. However, I happened to remember something from navigation school telling how this type of foggy weather usually did not go all the way down to the water. There tended to be about 400 feet of clear air between the surface of the sea and the fog. I suggested to the planning staff that we fly underneath the weather till close to the target. Near land the weather always lifted and we could take the formation over the top of some protecting hills along the coast, and drop right down on the unsuspecting Japanese to bomb from about 3,000 feet. Staff liked the idea, and we flew the last part of the mission about 300 feet off the water. That's tough duty—we had to pay attention to everything second to second.

Weather close to land did clear as expected and we pulled up just over the top of that ring of hills and were over the target before the Japs knew what was going on. They didn't get one Zero in the air. After dropping our bombs, our 50 millimeters raked buildings and Zeros on the ground unopposed. Actually, Myrtle's specific target was a building marked with a big red cross on its roof, meaning it was a hospital, which would put it off limits. However, intelligence had told us that it was not a hospital at all, but an ammunition dump. This was risky—if we attacked it and intelligence was wrong, that would be a gross violation of the rules of the Geneva Convention—not only might we be in trouble, but Tokyo Rose would have a field day. (Tokyo Rose spoke English without a trace of an accent on her nightly propaganda radio program beamed to forces throughout the South Pacific.) We were instructed to take that chance. Bombardier John Perry let go with a string of 500 pounders—one made a direct hit and the place blew into a thousand pieces amid fire and smoke. Hooray for Intelligence! Now the clouds were our friends—we climbed into them and were safely hidden almost immediately.

After that flight, Colonel Bill Miller asked me if I would stay on another three months when my 300-hour tour of duty was finished. He offered me the job of Group Navigation Officer, and though I was due an automatic Captaincy on November 1, he promised a promotion to Major one month later. That was pretty enticing, but there was a conflict – my sense of duty and the extra money for the promotions weighed against my loneliness for Betty and our baby son whom I had never seen.

CHAPTER 10

INTERLUDE IN ADELAIDE OR THE LULL BEFORE THE STORM

On September 1st, I finally got my upgrade to First Lieutenant and had about 140 hours of combat time toward the 300 necessary to qualify for stateside return to my beloved Betty. September didn't add many hours to the total because we flew only two missions and had to abort a third on account of engine trouble. A much-needed R&R, seven days in Adelaide on the south coast of Australia, also cut down our hours that month, but was worth it.

A mission to Ambon demonstrated graphically the importance of strict adherence to orders. Ambon was a little Jap-held island about 800 miles to the north with an important airbase and harbor. Our September 3rd orders were to attack harbor facilities there, specifically stating "DO NOT BOMB SHIPPING." When we came out of the clouds over the harbor, it was full of ships as expected. As we dove down to make our bomb run on the docks, we saw one huge transport lying at anchor. How tempting! Bombardier John Perry was dying to get it in spite of orders. It took a hasty and heated exchange to convince him otherwise. Finally he gave up, insisting that when we got home, we should at least learn the reason we had to pass up such a juicy target.

I was elected to find the answer to this frustrating question because in addition to being Squadron Navigation Officer, I had now become Intelligence Officer (more responsibility but no more pay). The latter job required me to get flight logs from each airplane returning from a mission, and to make a preliminary assessment of damage it had inflicted. I then reported my findings to Royal Australian Headquarters at Dawin and told them of our over-the-target argument to bomb or not to bomb shipping. They knew all about the tempting targets in the harbor. Six submarines had been dispatched to intercept that convoy after it left the harbor. Those ships would be sitting ducks for the sub's torpedoes, which were far more accurate than our bombs would have ever been. Too many 500-pound bombs had been wasted falling harmlessly into the sea—a bombardier would need incredible luck to hit a tiny ship from high altitude.

Ultimately, we learned that our subs sank 26 of those ships. Also the subs couldn't do the job on the docks that our bombs could. Knowing only part of the puzzle, we were not privy to the bigger picture as seen by high command. Result? After that there was no more questioning orders from Headquarters.

When debriefing after every mission was finished, all members of the crew got two shots of whiskey from the flight surgeon, compliments of the Aussies. What an incentive to get things wrapped up quickly on the way home!

Of course there were non-combat flights. On a trip to Fifth Air Force Headquarters in Brisbane, I flew as Colonel Bill Miller's navigator. Apparently some high-ranking official was expected about the time we arrived. When we landed, the tower thought we were the VIP flight and instructed us to taxi to the reviewing stand. Of course we followed orders. I happened to be first out of the plane. When Miller saw all the troops standing at attention, he called to me from the cockpit window, "Porky, give em at ease!" I barked out, "At ease!" As we were not the expected VIPs, we were directed to a less distinguished part of the field.

In Brisbane, Colonel Miller had reservations to stay at the hotel that MacArthur and other high-ranking officers used. Because of my lowly First Lieutenant rank, the hotel clerk said I couldn't stay there. Miller got really irritated and informed him, "He's my navigator and I never let a navigator out of my sight!" The desk clerk gave up as we would just stay overnight anyway. I appreciated Miller going to bat for me and my second-class citizenship. His support was probably part of his campaign to build personal rapport and convince me to stay on another three months.

As I've said before, South Pacific weather could be as much of an enemy as the Japs. Our copilot, Al Paris, agrees vehemently with me on this. Once coming back from a long mission, we encountered 150-mph headwinds that played hell with our gas mileage. As things became more critical, I started shooting two-star fixes (which were a lot faster to compute but not as accurate as the more tedious three-star fixes). Constantly updating our position, I was giving Farrington a series of one-degree corrections. Probably suspecting the worst, he finally asked me, "Bill, what the hell is going on? Why are you giving me all these minor corrections?"

I told him bluntly, "Because if we don't hit the field dead-on, we'll go in the drink about three miles offshore."

When we approached Darwin, we had so little gas we didn't dare fly the traffic pattern—we just flew straight on to the strip and touched down. When we reached the end of the runway, two of our four engines cut out.

On September 13, we got seven days leave, which meant a carefree vacation in civilization. Adelaide had not been an R&R stop and its city dads, feeling discriminated against, requested that Allied Headquarters put them on the leave circuit. Besides the good neighbor aspect, it would bring extra money into the city. We were the first servicemen to visit Adelaide, so the American Consul gave a party for us. During dinner, I met a young lady by the name of Katherine Rymill. She asked if I liked sports and I didn't disappoint her. I told her I was a sports fan, but fishing and golf were my favorites.

"I don't fish," said she, "but I play a little golf. Would you like to play tomorrow?"

How could I refuse an offer like that? She picked me up about 8 A.M. and we went out to the local club where the old caddy master fixed me up with a set of clubs. As we approached the first tee, I said, "Your honor," meaning that she should tee off first, but she declined sportingly enough, and insisted that we flip for it. She won the toss and started toward the men's tee. Thinking that she had made an error, I reminded her that the women's tee was ahead.

"I always use the blue tee," she replied sweetly, and hauled off and knocked the ball about 220 yards down the middle of the fairway. I knew then I was up against some tough competition. She continued to make those long drives, and her putting was something to behold. She wound up with a 73! Back at the clubhouse I remarked to the old caddy master, "Miss Rymill is a helluva golfer,"

He smiled at my ignorance and told me, "She's probably the best woman golfer we've ever had in Australia." Little did I know I'd been playing with the Australian Women's Champion!

Adelaide is a beautiful city located in an extensive grape, citrus, and truck farming region much like Southern California. People there are delightful and hospitable. Unlike most of the prominent cities on that continent, Adelaide had never been a penal colony for British convicts. When the American colonies won the Revolutionary War, thus depriving the English of their dumping ground for undesirables, they started shipping them 'down under.' Australia didn't like it any better than the Americans had, but as they were still beholden to England, they had to put up with it for about 80 years. Adelaide had the good luck to avoid the influx of convicts.

Like folks on the U.S. home front, Australia had gas rationing. Many motorists resorted to a charcoal burning device that generated a gas to power their vehicles. Even busses used it. Fortunately, we had the foresight to bring some five-gallon cans of 100-octane aviation gasoline. It could be used in their cars if cut with kerosene to keep it from burning up the motors. Between our gasoline and cigarettes, we had no lack of grateful friends to tour the city with, and enjoyed ourselves immensely.

Australians, like my wife, are avid horsemen. We went to an amateur horse race that offered 100 pounds to the winner. Shortly before the race, one of the jockeys became ill and the announcer asked if there were anyone there who could substitute for him. Our bombardier, John Perry, who had done a lot of riding, volunteered. Besides being handy with the Norden bombsight, he proved to be an able horseman and won the race. His additional funds added to our merriment in Adelaide.

Grapes grown in the mild Adelaide climate make excellent wine. Touring some of these wineries was an important part of our 'spiritual' education. Champagne and sparkling Burgundy have been produced in the U.S. for years, but the Aussies add their own touch by fizzing almost everything alcoholic. Sparkling Rhine wine and Moselle were two of their best.

When I returned from leave, two telegrams awaited me. One was from Betty, announcing the birth of our son, Bill III, on September 11, and the other from my father, which read "Congratulations on the birth of Bill III. You're so awkward, I never thought you'd make it." The paternal dig was because he was so handy with tools, which I was not. Mechanical aptitude has never been my strong suit. Being a new papa was great, but it seemed very strange being 8,000 miles away from the blessed event. I started signing letters to Betty "Bill Sr.," happily getting used to my new role in life.

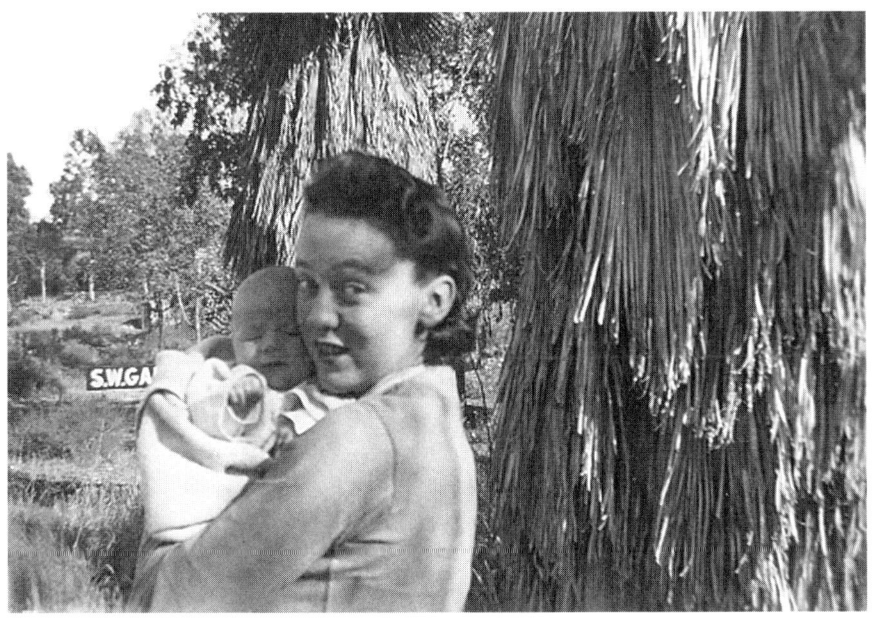

Bill McFerren III, born 9/11/43. His Daddy didn't learn about it until returning home from leave in Adelaide, September 20. When he grew up, he flew P-3s for the Navy in Vietnam.

Saturday
October ?th

My dear Betty—

It's a hellava note when one cannot remember the day of the month— I must be getting stale.

I feel a bit guilty – I've been intending to write since word was received of Bill Jr's arrival, but, as you know, some of us are inclined to be a bit lazy and are always putting it off until tomorrow. A great procrastinator – that's me all over.

Needless to say Bill is as proud as a peacock and as happy as a lark over the addition to the family. I might also add that yours truly adds his bit also. After all— an heir is quite an occasion – particularly a bouncing boy. The time element involved has its many amusing sidelights and Bill has been unmercifully teased about it.

As you know we were on leave when Bill Jr stepped into the world, so to properly celebrate the occasion we popped the corks on innumerable bottles of sparkling burgundy. As you might know the evening was quite successful – and all those who participated were of the mind that Bill Jr was duly set into this troubled world in the style befitting his parentage.

The heat is rapidly becoming unbearable and that calls for a swim, so rather than ramble on and say practically nothing – I'll close for now.

Again – I'm mighty proud of you – Betty

As ever,
John

CHAPTER 11

TERROR IN THE SKY

In October, General MacArthur's ground forces were in the final stages of planning an invasion of Japanese-held northern New Guinea. The General was a stickler for detail and insisted on the very latest dope on enemy strength and positions. On October 5, we made a recce mission to Sorong and neighboring islands. A few days later, we were sent to destroy oil storage and harbor facilities at Makassar on the southernmost tip of the Celebes. Moving closer, the 380th got orders to shift part of the Group north to Port Moresby at the far southeastern tip of New Guinea on the Coral Sea.

MacArthur wanted all the cards stacked in our favor when we made our big move. One of the reasons he was such a master tactician was that he left nothing to chance. He asked General Kenney's 5th Air Force to "bring everything you have" so as to mass our strength within easy striking distance of Rabaul, a major Japanese base supplying their forces in New Guinea and the Soloman Islands. Kenney got comittments from several U.S. groups for 86 aircraft plus what the Aussies could contribute. Fyrtle Myrtle and crew were among those sent by the 380th.

Leaving Manbaloo in the morning, we landed at Port Moresby in early afternoon, just in time to see a P-47 land. A pilot in civilian clothes got out. Curious, I asked the ground crew chief who in the world that could be.

"Why," said he, as though everybody ought to know the answer to that one, "that's Colonel Charles Lindberg."

"The hell it is!" I exclaimed, "What's he doing over here?"

"He works for Republic Aviation. They build P-47s and he's just been demonstrating how effective they are against the Zero. He just went up and shot down two of them."

In the Operations shack, I approached the famous flyer and asked, "Colonel Lindberg, can I speak to you for a moment?"

He smiled and said, "Sure you can, young man. What's on your mind?"

I told him, "I was out fishing in the creek in Illinois when I was twelve years old and the sirens in town began blowing on and on, so I hopped on my bike and beat it in to town to see what all the commotion was about. Everybody was celebrating because you'd just landed in Paris. And here only a few years later, you're out shooting down Zeros." He seemed to get a kick out of that, and it sure was a thrill for me to talk with him.

We flew to Rabaul five times in a row, but a persistent cloud cover thwarted us every time. Our greatest accomplishment was that we didn't run into each other in the soup! Our efforts to destroy Rabaul came to naught, and by October 20, we were back at Manbaloo.

Colonel Miller was still after me to stay on and become Group Navigation Officer after my 300 hours were up. While I was eager to get home to Betty and our new little son, this was war. When they praise you for your skill and they need you, it's hard to shirk responsibility. Then there was the matter of money. My only income was my First Lieutenant's pay. Betty's parents weren't rich, and it embarrassed me when they gave us a $1,000 check for a wedding present. That was a lot of money and I wanted to make it up to them. That figured in my reasoning about accepting the Colonel's offer. Of course my military status would benefit from promotion to Captain, then Major, which would come with a new job. Two days before we got shot down, I told him I'd stay.

Our target on October 26, 1943, was Pomelaa, a nickel refinery on the main Celebes island. It supplied over half of the nickel needed to make alloys necessary for aircraft production. Plans called for twelve planes, six from Fenton and six from Manbaloo.

The trip began uneventfully enough, although the Fenton six never joined us for a variety of reasons. Two from our Manbaloo

Relentless pounding of the Celebes

Group aborted with mechanical problems, leaving less than half of the intended strength to complete the job and defend ourselves.

We reached the target area, and with no resistance from the ground, dropped our bombs and with two other crews were ready to form up and get the hell out of there. However a fourth plane, the Golden Gator, had broken discipline contrary to orders that plainly stated, "Do not bomb shipping." (Same as Ambon—we had submarines in the area just waiting for ships to leave the harbor.) The Gator was still dawdling around trying to bomb a ship as the minutes ticked off. We were increasingly exposed to attack by fighters based only 100 miles away at Kendari as a result of his uncalled-for actions.

This was our first mission without Al Paris as he had been promoted to Captain of another crew. Our new copilot was Tracy DuMont, who, though he had previous multi-engine time, was on his first mission on a B-24. This whole situation made me extremely apprehensive, especially since the Golden Gator pilot had received two reprimands for hot-rodding his plane, being taken off flying status for two months the second time he did it.

John Farrington called the Golden Gator on the 522 set (plane-to-plane radio) and told its pilot to forget his one-man heroics and get back in formation, "So we can get the hell out of here before the Zeros show up."

An answer crackled back, "Mind your own business. I'm going to get that sucker."

"John," I warned, "we can't afford the time over the target. Let the SOB go and let's get outta here."

Living up to his nickname of Mother, John ignored me, hoping to provide protection for the maverick and his crew. We circled for about 25 minutes which was 25 minutes too long as far as our crew was concerned.

By now I was so furious with John for letting one would-be hero showoff endanger all the rest of us including his own crew, I literally screamed at him, "I just got married and have a little baby. I'll be damned if I'm going to lose my life because somebody deliberately screwed up a mission!" It did no good. We had already lost precious minutes. If Al had been there in the right-hand seat, I know he would have backed me up.

Finally, we headed home in a loose diamond formation. Myrtle was in the number two slot on the left. I had begun to think the impossible just might happen and maybe we wouldn't get jumped by fighters after all. We had started to eat lunch when a dozen Zeros came in from dead ahead. Canon fire hit our nose, killing John Perry, bombardier, and James DeGroat, nose gunner, and fatally wounding John Farrington. The nosewheel hydraulic reservoir was on fire. I was on the flight deck right behind Farrington. I quickly ducked behind one of the armored plates, which probably saved my life. Howard Sleighter and I tried to put out the fire but it had too much of a head start. I could see our beloved Myrtle was doomed. Her pilot was dying—his last audible words were, "Tell the others to go home. They can't help us now." We were down to about 3,000 feet, losing altitude rapidly in a shallow but irreversible dive. Smoke filled the cabin. I realized that it was up to me now as senior officer to take command. I sent Sleighter back to the waist to tell everyone to bail out.

When I went back up on the flight deck, that gutsy Louis Glavin was still firing away from the top turret. I reached up and slapped him on the leg and yelled, "Louie, we gotta get outta here. BAIL OUT" He came down from his position, and we opened the top escape hatch and signaled Tracy DuMont, the green copilot to jump. Partway out of the hatch, Tracy froze. Lou Glavin and I each took one of his feet and flipped him out, hollering not to forget to pull the ripcord. Glavin went out next but was never seen again. He could have been hit by part of the tail section or, if he made it out, he could have become entangled in the shrouds of his chute, or sharks could have gotten him. Immediately after Lou, I climbed up into the hatch. Just as I did, the plane blew up and I was in the air, dazed and in free fall, maybe 500 feet above the water.

Just in time, I came to my senses enough to remember that I had to pull the rip cord. The chute opened just like it was supposed to—about the only thing that went right that day. It was one o'clock on a beautiful afternoon. As I drifted down, the sudden quiet and peacefulness was overwhelming, I thought, "Oh God, is this my last day on this earth?" But the Zeros didn't strafe me as they had been known to do. When I hit the water, I went down deep. I worried about being tangled in the parachute shrouds, so as soon as I could find them, I grabbed the front snaps and released the chute and kicked away from it. Then I pulled the cord on my Mae West (the popular term for the busty looking inflatable yellow life vest), which shot me up to the surface. The water was smooth and I spotted two life rafts—somehow when the plane blew up, the rafts had deployed and automatically inflated. It seemed like it took an hour for me to swim to them, especially because I was dragging my survival kit with me. It contained necessary items—fishing line, hooks, first aid things, and a little food.

As I got closer, I saw that Tracy was already in one of the rafts. After helping toss him out of our stricken plane, I was relieved to see that he had regained his composure enough to pull the ripcord. However he was still somewhat dazed when I got to the raft. I laboriously handed him my prized survival kit that had been such a drag on my swim. He took it and heaved it over his shoulder, but it didn't land in the raft as he intended. Instead it flew right across the raft and went to the bottom of the sea! Just an accident, of course, but what a bummer! As things turned out, it didn't make any difference. Once in the raft, I looked around and tried to get my bearings. I figured we were not too far from the prearranged rendezvous point, which is a different location on every mission. If a downed flyer is lucky enough to make it there, a submarine is supposed to show up and rescue him in about a week.

Though I suffered superficial scalp burns and bruises, I felt lucky to be relatively uninjuried and in good enough shape to paddle. Heading back for land, we towed the second raft in case we might run across guys that had bailed out ahead of us. Survivors could be scattered over five miles of ocean, since at a speed of 120 miles an hour our crippled plane had covered about two miles every minute before crashing.

Sleighter and the crew had jumped a few minutes before Glavin, Dumont, and me. I estimated we were about 12 miles from land and 900 miles from home. We had probably put about 100 miles between us and the target we had just bombed.

By now it was around 2 P.M. of the longest afternoon of my life. Soon we sighted a patrol boat bearing down on us. The Nips had, of course, alerted their coastal patrol to look for two downed B-24 crews, They were eager to get their hands on live members of the bomber group that had been harassing them so unmercifully these many months. They knew we had important information, which they intended to extract from us any way they could.

As the patrol boat approached, I began to check my pockets to make sure I didn't have anything they might want. The only thing I found was a letter from my wife written September 11 only a few hours after the birth of our son. She had scrawled, "We had Bill III today. Honey, it wasn't too bad. It was like falling off a high bar." I had kept that letter with me ever since I received it, but because it bore her address, I tore it up and pitched it into the sea.

The patrol boat was well-armed with canon and machine guns. I pulled out my 45 to toss it overboard and DuMont (still not thinking too clearly) asked in panic, "What are we gonna do, shoot it out with 'em?"

I said, "Tracy, don't be a nut. They've got heavy armament. I just want to get rid of this thing so they won't think we're hostile and fire on us."

I was about to become a prisoner of war just as I had dreamed only two nights before and told Betty about in my October 24 letter. I was beginning two years of physical, mental, and emotional hell.

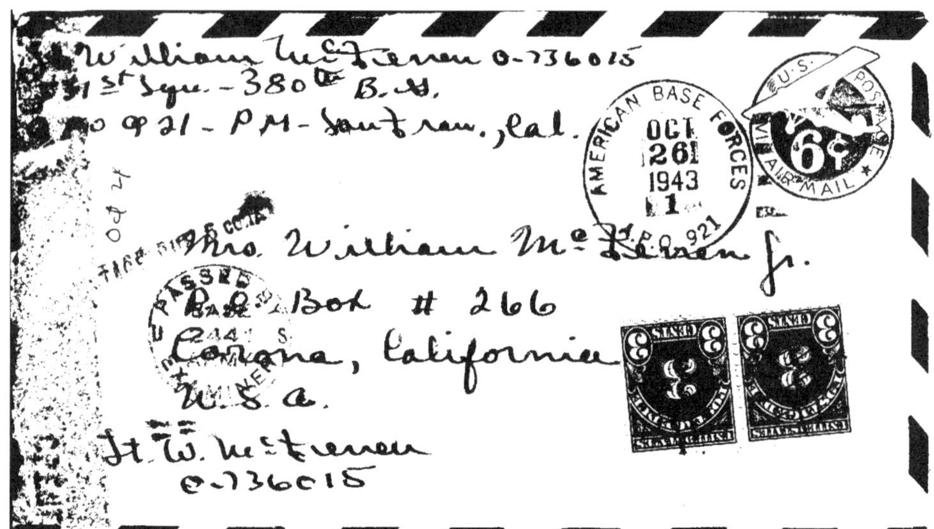

William McKiernan 0-736015
531st Sqn. - 380th B.G.
APO 921 - PM - San Fran., Cal.

AMERICAN BASE FORCES
OCT 26 1943
A.P.O. 921

U.S. POSTAGE
VIA AIR MAIL
6¢

Mrs. William McKiernan Jr.
P.O. Box # 266
Corona, California
U.S.A.

PASSED BY ARMY EXAMINER

Lt. W. McKiernan
0-736015

①   Sunday, Oct. 24, 1943

Betty darling -

The weather has been so hot that I just couldn't write yesterday, as I was dripping wet all day - a poor excuse but that's the way things go. I shall try not to let it happen again.

I had a lousy dream last nite - it was the most realistic I ever had - I dreamt I had been captured by the Japs, and boy, was I glad when I woke up on my downy white couch - our tent seemed like a palace. I shall have to be more discriminating in the future so far as my dreams are concerned.

CHAPTER 12

A ONE WAY TICKET TO JAPAN

A million thoughts flooded through my mind as the Japanese patrol boat bore down on Tracy and me. Standard belief among our people was whether you were captured or killed, it amounted to the same thing. Always the optimist and skeptical of rumor, I didn't know what to expect. I chose to believe that essential decency of human beings, even in wartime, would prevail. As they approached us, my philosophizing gave way to coping with the minute-to-minute situation and hoping for the best.

When the boat came alongside, a couple of seamen dropped a ladder and beckoned to us to climb up. They stripped us to our skivies and sat us down beside the bulkhead where they could keep an eye on us. None of them spoke English. After the officers went below to eat, one of the sailors motioned for me to stand up. He hauled off and hit me in the nose. My nose is especially sensitive because I had three operations on it before the days of seatbelts. In pain and anger, I responded instinctively and knocked him to the deck. I used to box when I was at Yale and when he got up, I hit him again. That was a huge mistake. The other sailors joined the fray and beat the hell out of me. I came to my senses and realized that it was not a level playing field. That was the last time I hit any Jap.

Finally we were given tea and a couple of rice balls, and left for the night, practically naked. We damn near froze to death.

The next morning the ship docked at Kendari, which I recognized because we had bombed it on a previous mission. We were put in a jail where the voice of an unseen guard spoke to me in English. "I have a wife in Los Angeles. Do you think she's okay?"

Hoping to win a friend, and not knowing anything at all about his wife, I tried to give a reassuring answer, saying something about how decent and fair Americans were and not to worry. He might have heard about the U.S. rounding up Japanese-American families, forcing them to sell California real estate at fire-sale prices, and resettling them in concentration camps. After the war when I learned of this atrocious action against American citizens, it appalled me. Lots of Japanese-Americans served with distinction in American forces in North Africa, and though it was hush-hush, many served in the Pacific as translators and in Intelligence.

The next day, the fighter pilots who shot us down came to see us, an eerie situation. One asked in good English, "What do you think of Japanese pilots?" That was a no-brainer. I replied, "They're damn good. They shot us down."

Actually, I did have respect for Japanese pilots, and tried to flatter them a little. It paid off because in return for the compliments, they gave me a package of cigarettes, which were terrible but better than no cigarettes at all.

Two days later, I heard familiar voices. Lardin, Sleighter, and Lovett had made it to an island where they arranged with the natives for a boat and provisions to take them back to Australia. (Long before the war, Aussies had traded with the islanders and there was a friendly network in existence.) The boys had charts appropriate for the trip and all systems were 'go,' but not long after their departure, they were intercepted at sea and taken to Kendari, where they wound up in cells adjacent to DuMont and myself.

John Lardin told me he didn't have his Mae West on when we ditched. He and Sleighter were competitive long-distance swimmers and managed to swim eight miles to shore. John said that after he had been swimming a couple of hours, he looked back and saw a big shark following him. He never looked back again, just kept swimming.

Two men were still missing, Louis Glavin, our top turret gunner, and Dan Glendon, one of our waist gunners. No one but the sharks would know what happened to them.

Now interrogation started and lasted all day. Dumont and I followed standard procedure and told them this was our first mission, which was partially true—it was Dumont's first, but my 18th. Primarily they wanted to know where the escape point was because they knew that it was a pre-arranged spot where downed flyers and rescuers would attempt to rendezvous. Unfortunately, we had a photographer onboard that day who was not a regular member of our crew. I had never met or ever seen him before because when he boarded the plane, I was busy with my pre-flight weather briefing. The first time I laid eyes on him was after we were in prison. I knew we were in trouble when that photographer told them things they wanted to hear. It was he who spilled the beans about a designated escape point. I don't know what possessed him to tell them that only the pilot and navigator knew its location. (Actually our whole crew knew about the escape point.) The Japs quickly recognized a willing stool pigeon and flew the photographer to Tokyo for what I assumed would be red carpet treatment. At least I never crossed paths with that gentleman again.

Since John Farrington, our pilot, was dead, the Japanese focused on me to get the information they wanted. When I refused to talk, they started to beat me in the groin and otherwise torment me. After all that, it was hard to manage the composure to point out that I was not privy to rescue information after sending off a distress signal. I told them our forces might search for us by air, or by sea where we had ditched. I told them I couldn't know about all the prearranged escape point locations since it would not be practical to establish them to cover all ditching possibilities. Since I was an officer, the rank-conscious Japanese believed me for the moment and let up. They had previously learned that either a PBY flying boat or a submarine would arrive at our escape point one week later to look for survivors. The area where we went down was within sight of Japanese-held territory so the Japs correctly assumed it would be a submarine.

A day or two later they decided that I must know more than I let on so they tried the ultimate psychological ploy. I was taken from my cell and tied to a tree. A squad of six Jap soldiers armed with rifles marched in with an officer who said that I was going to be shot unless I told them what they wanted to know. He 'iced' the situation by giving me a last cigarette and a drink so I would have time to think about it.

I didn't give a damn about myself any longer. I figured I was as good as dead. I resolved not to endanger the lives of 90 submariners who also had mothers, fathers, sweethearts or wives. As a military man you know what you have to do when it's your life or 90 others, so I said good-bye to my wife and my family and my son whom I had never seen. The officer again asked me where the escape point was, and I again told him I didn't know. He ordered them to cock their rifles. I thought, "If I'm going to die, I'm at least going to do so with pride and self respect." Then the officer made a downward motion with his arm, but they didn't fire. This was repeated three times. The whole episode probably took only minutes but it seemed to me like hours. After the war, I learned that a similar procedure took place with another 380th crew they had captured. I don't know about those guys, but I have never been so scared in all my life.

The next day they decided to try Plan B since intimidation had failed. I was brought before a high-ranking officer who was introduced to me as an Admiral. He was a smallish man in his forties who spoke perfect English. He greeted me courteously and asked the guard to bring me some clean clothes 'so I would be more comfortable.' Now I was dressed in clean khaki shirt and pants, and I must admit it felt better. The Admiral became very apologetic, hoping to lull me into a sense of false security I guess. He said, "I am very upset that you have been mistreated. It won't happen again while I'm here," then began to question me. Again I said I didn't know the answers.

He ordered some food, and hoping to catch me off guard asked, "Do you like Sake?"

I answered that I liked almost anything with alcohol in it, and that got a laugh out of him.

He invited, "Why don't you and I drink a little Sake together?" An aide delivered a quart bottle for each of us, and we started conversing in pleasantries about sports, fishing, and other non-controversial subjects. What he didn't know was that I had a high tolerance for alcohol. Even Betty's Uncle Clayton had been amazed at the amount I could put away without showing it. After every mission, in addition to the two shots issued by the Aussies, I usually consumed my share of scotch or vodka at the O club.

As we neared the bottom of our Sake bottles, he suggested we might have more. As if by magic, two full bottles appeared. The Admiral's speech was becoming a bit slurred, and he was having trouble finding the right words to express himself. After we had put serious dents in our second bottles, he became very wobbly while gamely carrying on with the charade. It wasn't long before he passed out completely. There were three aides present, and when their boss folded, they couldn't contain their embarrassment. They took back the clean clothes, kicked me in the groin for good measure, and threw me back in jail. My attitude was as though it had been somewhat of a sporting event won by me, and I figured at least one Nip had learned a lesson about drinking with an American.

After 19 days in the Kendari jail, a truck took us to Pomela. I wondered if they were taking us there to execute us since that had been one of our targets. When we arrived we could see the damage we had inflicted on the nickel mine. Apparently we missed the power plant tower as it was still standing. Bombing in those days was not as precise as it is today—a 300-pound bomb could easily miss the target by as much as 100 yards.

My fears of execution diminished as we were loaded on a small ship for a day's sail to Makassar, another of our targets on the south part of the main Celebes island. When we got there, our old 380th Group flew over and bombed us. Fortunately we couldn't personally be blamed for that attack. There was a P-38 pilot in jail there at Makassar who had been shot down at Babo. He was able to confirm that our Babo target, which had caused us so much consternation, was indeed not a hospital but a big ammo dump. That really made me feel good.

They held us about four days at Makassar then put us on a ship for another of our previous targets—Balikpapan—the oil refinery we had bombed twice and received a decoration for. While on that ship, we were guarded by an older Chief Petty Officer who treated us well and would not allow anyone to hit us. At Balikpapan, we were put in a former Dutch jail for about three weeks while the ship was undergoing repairs and taking on a cargo of bauxite. The food was terrible and you had to relieve yourself through a small hole in the floor. It got to be one awful stench in that jail.

Finally we were put back on the boat with destination Singapore. Praise be, the same decent Chief Petty Officer was in charge. I found out that he had been at Annapolis long before the war when the Japanese government had donated and planted cherry trees there. He liked Americans. I told him I didn't think the war was a good idea, to which he agreed. Second day out, a sailor made the mistake of hitting me in the face in the presence of the Chief, knocking me down. The Chief grabbed the man and beat the hell out of him. Word must have gotten around because that was the last time anyone hit us while he was in charge. Actually the best treatment I ever got from the Japanese anywhere was on that ship.

On Christmas Day, 1943, we arrived at Singapore. I was up on deck for the customary afternoon tea when the Chief sent for me. When I arrived at his quarters, he was sitting on a mat with a bottle of whisky. I didn't know what to think. It was not the common drink, Sake, but actual honest-to-God whiskey—an extreme luxury in the Orient. That told me that he wanted this moment to be a special one. He got up, shook hands with me, and said, "Today is Christmas. Let's you and I have a drink together." Obviously he was having ambivalent feelings. He ordered some food and we spent a few precious moments discussing things as you might at a cocktail party, momentarily transcending the fact that we were mortal enemies at war with one another. When we had finished our food and drink and chit chat, he said somewhat self-consciously, "Now get out of here. Christmas is Christmas and war is war." I thanked him for the pleasant interlude and left.

Our boat sailed from Singapore bound for Japan across the East China Sea in a convoy of eleven transports and four escort vessels. I was on deck one afternoon three days out when one of the ships, only about 300 yards away, blew up, obviously hit by a torpedo. In short order, I heard others explode—American submarines on the attack! I hardly knew how to react when this happened. I didn't want to die, but I got a real charge out of seeing the destruction the enemy was sustaining. The ship I was on had a narrow escape when a torpedo passed by close to the stern. What was left of our convoy turned back to Singapore where we picked up another convoy and once more set sail for what turned out to be an uneventful trip to Japan.

I would look at the moon at night and think that it was the one thing Betty and I had in common. She told me later that she did the same.

Finally we reached a southern Japanese port during the night and the six of us were loaded on a train. It seemed my tour of enemy-held ports was nearing an end. I was briefly grateful, unaware that the next chapter would be the lowest of low points for a POW—Ofuna, an interrogation camp about thirty miles Southwest of Tokyo. I arrived there January 2, 1944—my first wedding anniversary. What a way to spend a day that under different circumstances would have been a cause for celebration! Sometime during all this trauma, I can't say exactly when, I had made up my mind that <u>I was going to pull through</u>. No matter what was in store for me, I <u>would</u> get back to Betty and my young son. I would do whatever it took to survive (consistent, of course, with military expectations and my own personal sense of honor).

On the home front, two months before, Betty had received the dreaded Missing-In-Action telegram from the War Department. It came on November 2, which was just a week after we were shot down. The bad news traveled quickly to my family and friends. Betty received many letters of consolation and support. Bravely she continued to write to me in hopes I would be found, so I would have mail from home awaiting my return. But even her gallant 'chin up' attitude had to wane when her letters started being returned to her marked 'Missing-in-Action.'

Following is a copy of a letter she wrote two days after receiving the MIA telegram. She sent it to *Mademoiselle Magazine*, which published it and paid her $50. She saw an ad in the paper about a Royal typewriter for sale for $50. A perfect match! She still uses that old typewriter and refuses to exchange it for a modern one.

Mademoiselle, March 1944

TONIGHT WILL BE DIFFERENT

Excerpts from a letter written by Betty McFerren to her husband, William, who was reported missing in action somewhere in the Southwest Pacific.

My darling –

Today my morale has risen. Your love is giving me strength across those eight thousand miles of water. Although the message said "missing in action," you are alive somewhere and some day will laugh at those empty words. We will laugh at them together one of these days.

Memories—they're a miserable substitute for the real thing, but, oh, so precious to me now. Those weekends when you were a navigation cadet in Sacramento—the dances at the Senator, the steaks and spaghetti at Julia's, the lobster at the Grotto. And all the time it seemed to me some kind of miracle that I'd actually found you.

Our crazy wedding! And our wedding night in San Francisco, with every stitch of my trousseau in the checkroom of that Sacramento hotel. Taking our wedding cake on the troop train with ninety-three other newly graduated navigators, eight wives and one wife-to-be.

Your phone call that Easter Sunday night to announce the extra week in California. Our seven unbroken days together twenty-four hours a day—and no getting up at the break of dawn to reach the field in time, no staggering in dead tired at midnight after a twelve-hour grind. Just time—and you. Races at Bay Meadows, lunch at Fisherman's Wharf, riding the cable cars, dancing at the St. Francis, and that last short weekend in the country.

Blue Monday had to come, of course. I did not expect our parting to be easy. It wasn't. All day I was conscious that each minute you were farther and farther away from me somewhere out over the Pacific.

It does seem to me now that we lived a lifetime in those seven months. Not only because of what we did together, where we went, what we saw, but what we thought. We understood each other so completely. We were so completely happy.

Darling, our sweet child is two months old today and I am glad he is beginning to look like you. I must not keep the light on much longer for it may wake him. Last night and the night before I hoped I would dream of you. But sleep must come before dreams may start.

Tonight, though, will be different. Tonight, while I have been writing this to you, you have been with me—here in this room. And now your love is making me strong, and mine is going out to you to bring you safely home. Tonight I know your love will always make me strong.

Goodnight darling. Here is my love, tonight and always.

— Betty

All the letters she had mailed to me before she knew I had been shot down, and after, were returned. She thrust them aside in grief, unopened. They remained neatly tied in bundles for 52 years until discovered in our basement in the spring of 1995. It would be an understatement to say that reading them rekindled old emotions that I had thought long forgotten. Those traumatic and wonderful times came alive again and left me with tears flowing copiously.

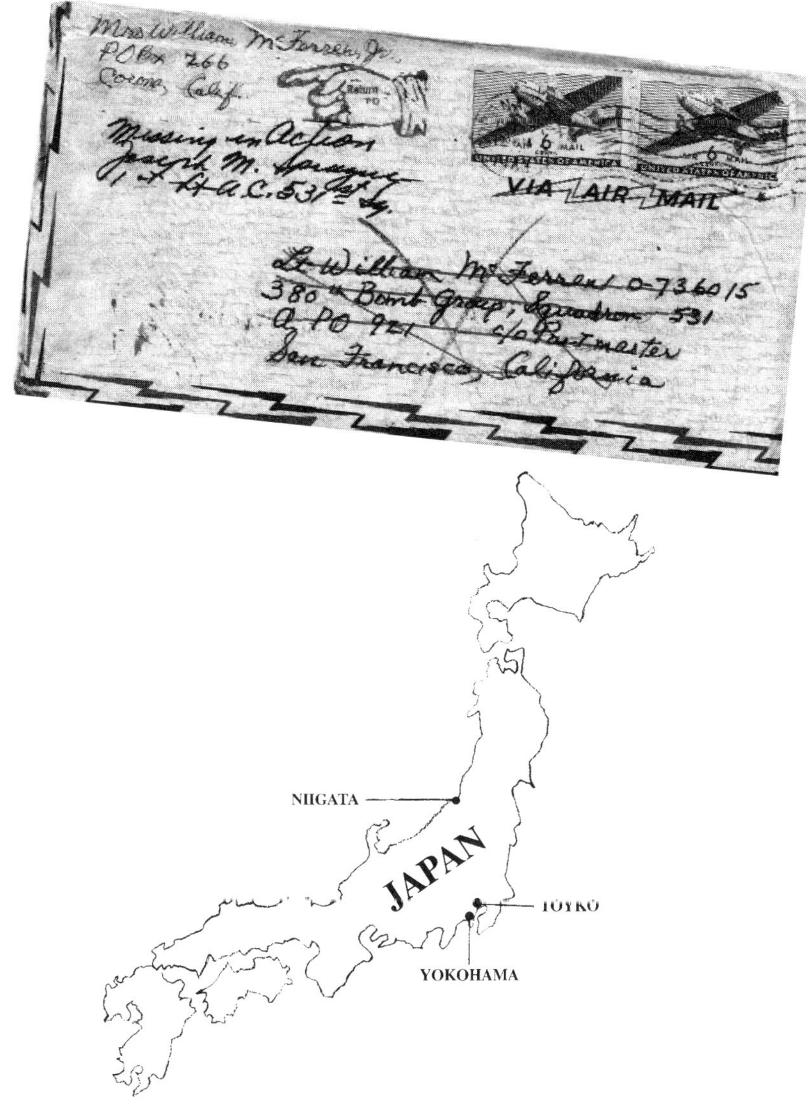

CHAPTER 13

THE GENEVA CONVENTION

Editor's Note: I have been advised to either omit this chapter or relocate it as an appendix, but it seems so relevant to me that I have elected to leave it here.

A puzzling thing to me is the idealism of devising certain niceties or "Rules of War" in an attempt to lessen war's unmitigated violence, Nevertheless in 1864, with laudable foresight, a number of civilized nations met in Geneva, Switzerland, and agreed to try. They signed a pact called "The Geneva Convention," and in ensuing years added refinements. It was, of course, far from 100% effective, but it may well be that some POWs survived because of some slight benefits received. Any country holding prisoners had to be aware that if the tables were turned, some benefit might accrue to their own fighting men. This aspect is questionable, however, in light of the Japanese belief that allowing yourself to be taken prisoner is so disgraceful that you'd be better off dead.

Rules required a minimum of humanity—prisoners must be given food, shelter, and clothing comparable to that of the armed forces of their captors. When questioned, a prisoner was only required to give his name, rank, and serial number, and execution was forbidden. Officers could not be forced to work. Japan was a signatory to these rules so its leaders should have been well aware of them. However, in the war's early stages, the Japanese, flushed with victory after victory in the South Pacific, gave little thought to the possibility of losing the war and having to answer to a dominant power for their transgressions. Troops in the trenches, so to speak, felt free to ignore Geneva's rules. The Japs that tied me to that tree, execution style, certainly couldn't have cared less about rules of war! Though on second thought, they didn't shoot.

There were times, however, when failing to adhere to the rules was unavoidable. For instance, when the Island of Corregedor in the Philippines fell, and the Bataan Peninsula surrendered, the enemy was suddenly faced with caring for 60,000 prisoners. A section of the Treaty provides that captured personnel must be removed from the combat area ASAP.

The Japanese were unprepared for such possibility and had no way of dealing with it, with or without Geneva rules. They had no transportation for thousands of men, so the hungry and thirsty prisoners were forced to walk 70 miles over rough terrain in the infamous Bataan Death March. About ten thousand died from starvation or mistreatment. Guards thought nothing of bayoneting men who staggered and fell. Ameil Palermo, a doctor who became a close friend of mine in POW camp, survived Bataan, and after the war, Betty and I saw a great deal of him and his wife, Anita, out in the San Francisco Bay area.

The Japanese were amazed that Allied prisoners wanted their families to know of their capture. The prevailing Nipponese slant on this, especially among the younger ones, was, "Why would any fighting man disgrace himself and his family by admitting that he had allowed himself to be taken prisoner?" In my opinion, this conviction that death was preferable to dishonor had been drilled into the younger men by the military regime of the 1930s. It did not seem to be embraced quite so wholeheartedly by older soldiers, perhaps from the wisdom that comes with age. Be that as it may, since the idea of being taken prisoner was so repugnant to the rank and file of the military, no wonder they held the 'cowardly' (but still alive) prisoners in such contempt. This difference between Eastern and Western attitudes may have accounted in part for the insufferable treatment by our captors. The exception was a very few somewhat more humane men, who may have had more exposure to Western ways through education, travel or religion. The quite decent Chief Petty Officer on the boat to Japan who invited me to have a Christmas drink with him illustrates this point perfectly.

I learned later that as soon as the atrocities endured by Allied prisoners came to light, a storm of international indignation arose. Nipon (Dai Nipon meaning 'great Japan' was the way they referred to their country) began to realize there was a possibility they might lose the war and could be indicted under the War Crimes Act. This must have been the reason that in the war's later stages, we began to get a bit more food.

Understand though, that the problem of short rations applied not only to us—the Nips were hungry too. You never saw a fat Jap. Another reason that prisoner's food was so scarce was that the guards stole most of our Red Cross supplements. Testimony at the War Crimes Trials brought out that though no one had actually seen the guards take our packages, empty Red Cross cans and cartons were found by POWs on cleanup detail in the guards' sleeping rooms. Guards were also seen smoking American cigarettes. POWs were supposed to get a Red Cross package every week—I received only three the entire twenty-three months I was there!

CHAPTER 14

IN ENEMY HANDS - OFUNA

The first POW camp that I set foot in was Ofuna, which in peacetime had been the Hollywood of Japan, but Camp Ofuna, run by the navy, was anything but a glamorous film capitol. It was a disease-ridden hellhole. Medical attention was non-existent and outrageous cruelty was condoned, as shown by official testimony of B-24 pilot Loren Stoddard at the War Crimes Trials in San Francisco in December 1947. His plane was based at Kwajelein in the Marshall islands and was shot down late in May 1944, about 40 miles from Jap-held Saipan. His bombardier, 1st Lt. Ernest Peschau suffered severe abdominal injuries in the crash, which left him in such bad shape that he was unable to have a bowel movement. Survivors drifted in their life raft for four days, finally washing ashore on Saipan where they were taken prisoner. A week after the crash, the bombardier still hadn't received medical treatment and was in intense pain. When they were flown to Ofuna, he had to be carried, and in response to the Americans' request for medical help, the Chief Pharmacists Mate, who seemed to be in charge, only laughed. This was Kitamura, the 'quack,' well known for his brutality.

The dying man was carried to a 5-foot by 8-foot receiving cell and laid on the cement floor. His crew members tried to feed him some watery soup and rice but he was unable to eat. Repeated requests for pain pills or any sort of relief were ignored, and at about 7 P.M. on June 8, never having received so much as a pill or a shot to ease his suffering, Lt. Peschau died. I know for a fact that medicine was available 25 miles away at a hospital in Shinagawa where three captured American surgeons had been put in charge. Little good it did his unfortunate victims when

Kitamura was sentenced to four years at hard labor by the War Crimes Tribunal after the war, about 50 years too few as far as I was concerned.

The camp doctor at Ofuna was a real bastard—we saw a number of people die from neglect and malnutrition. The International Red Cross inspected periodically and reported a severe shortage of sulfa and other medications, along with widespread malnutrition and just plain starvation, but the reports did no good. Antibiotics were not widely used then, having only been recently invented. Penicillin was outrageously expensive. A secret method was discovered to collect and recycle it from urine, but it was used mainly for venereal disease.

At the War Crimes Trials, Captain Stoddard testified of atrocities inflicted upon Lts. Harris and Bullard when they were found looking at a hand drawn map of the Pacific Theater. They were severely beaten across the buttocks with a six-foot wooden club for 15 or 20 minutes. When Lt. Harris fell to the ground, Kitamura kicked him, screaming at him to get up until he staggered to his feet only to have Kitamura beat his face with his fists. He must have gotten some ungodly satisfaction from such atrocious behavior. When Lt. Harris fell again, Kitamura ordered Lt. Bullard to be brought from his cell where he was lying sick with dysentery and beriberi. Guards dragged him outside and stood him in front of Kitamura who beat him across the buttocks with his club, knocking him to the ground. The Americans were then ordered to carry him back to his cell. Kitamura drew a circle on the ground and ordered Lt. Harris to stand inside it until next mealtime.

Both men were in a state of semi-consciousness for a week, but they were made to carry on the daily cleanup routine and exercise. Pappy Boyington was one of several witnesses to this.

I'll never forget my first night at Ofuna. A voice from the next cell whispered through the thin wall. "Hey, you, over there, are you a new prisoner?" Cautiously, I answered, "Yeah, who are you?"

The voice replied, "I'm Greg Boyingon. Just call me Pappy." He explained that he was a Marine pilot, shot down in China. He arrived at Ofuna about a month before I did. He told me to say that I was on my first mission and to pretend that I didn't know much. That sounded easy. Pappy said that forms were used in questioning and to just give arbitrary numbers, but to be sure to remember what I'd said.

When 'Handsome Harry,' who spoke perfect English, began interrogation about how many planes were at Hickham Field, how many at Canton Island, how many at Brisbane, etc., I took Pappy's good advice and said there were about 200 at each base, which seemed to satisfy him. After that I was questioned about once a week. Apparently they were trying to see if I would forget what I had said the week before so they could catch me in a lie, which would be an excuse for a beating, which was their favorite sport. Fortunately, I have a good memory and didn't trip up.

Boyington, from Washington State, was the famous Ace who commanded the 'Black Sheep' Squadron. (An Ace is a fighter pilot with five kills to his credit.) He received the Medal of Honor for shooting down 24 Zeros before his luck ran out. Pappy and I became good friends. The last time I saw him was at an air show near Denver when Betty and I had the honor of his company for dinner at our house that night. He had been at the air show to promote his book, *Baa Baa Black Sheep*. Unfortunately Pappy never gave up his tobacco habit that had gotten him in trouble at Ofuna and contributed to terminal lung cancer.

I was also a smoker back then. One day I stole a cigarette from a guard's sleeping quarters while they were outside praising the Emperor. I gave Pappy half of it and he ducked in the latrine to have a smoke. A guard by the name of Yamazaki came in and caught him. Lt. Stoddard's testimony reveals what happened next. Yamakazi and another Guard named Ataki struck Pappy across his behind with a heavy wooden club at least ten times as hard as they could swing it. When they finished, he was made to stand at attention in one spot for the rest of the day, without food, water, or a chance to relieve himself. Witnesses to this were Lou Zamparini, the famous miler from the 1936 Olympics and my friend, Lt. Colonel Jim Walker. The Japs respected Pappy, though—when they beat him he would never utter a sound.

As I reviewed testimony that some of us gave after the war concerning the outrageous brutality by the guards, a curious fact came out. One American officer testified that before being questioned, he received a slip of paper that read, "You are not a prisoner of war but an unarmed enemy, and your position here can be regarded as an extension of hostilities. If you behave well and answer questions properly, your treatment will be governed accordingly and as well as existing regulations permit. The safety of your life is not guaranteed."

I personally did not receive such a notice, but whoever contrived such legal-sounding obfuscation probably thought they were cleverly dodging provisions of the Geneva Convention. How many allied prisoners were so warned I don't know, but clearly it was intended to absolve prison camp personnel of whatever might happen to their 'unarmed' enemy! Of course it was blatantly illegal, but that was not of any help to prisoners.

Discipline among the Japanese themselves was very harsh. When a Camp Commander entered the compound, everyone—Jap guards and POWs alike—had to stand at attention and salute him. One time we gave the necessary obeisance, but the guards, not expecting company, were still in the barracks drinking tea and playing cards. The Commander screamed for them and they came peeling out to stand at attention before him. He was so furious that he pulled out his gun and struck the first one on the head as hard as he could, which, unfortunately for the guard, killed him. Early-on Camp Commanders held only a rank no higher than sergeant, but with progress of the war, officialdom became more aware of the terrible mistreatment of prisoners. They were beginning to realize that victory for Japan was not a lead pipe cinch, and it was thought that officers might be more responsible, so the sergeants were replaced by officers as camp commanders. They had to be rotated frequently though since it wasn't considered appropriate duty for men of higher rank. None of the camps had many guards—they really didn't need many—a Caucasian couldn't get far in an escape attempt in oriental Japan.

But I am getting ahead of my story—when I arrived at Ofuna (I can hardly say the word Ofuna without my stomach tying in knots), I found myself with about 150 fellow prisoners—American, British, Canadian and Australian and some civilians from work crews on Wake Island. At first all ranks and nationalities mingled and bunked together, but later they separated us by rank. They told us it was to allow prisoners to separate themselves in orderly hierarchies, each group with its own senior representative to report to the camp commander. It was supposed to encourage a sense of self-discipline among us, but I suspected that the real reason was that they hoped it would make administration easier, while also preventing a certain amount of communication between prisoners.

A POW's day began at dawn. No matter what the weather, we had to assemble in ranks outdoors, get counted, and participate in bowing to the emperor. Once during this farce, I muttered softly for my buddy's ears only, "I hope you die, you son-of-a-bitch." Everyone laughed like hell. The guards couldn't figure out what was so funny, so rather than appear dumb, they laughed too.

Next came breakfast consisting of bean paste soup. Period. Dinner was rice or barley (rice was preferable). After I finished my barley, I felt like I should neigh and get ready for the fifth race at Hialeah. If we were lucky, there were fish heads in the soup and sometimes daikons, which are like coarse tasteless white carrots. Occasionally produce markets in the U.S. stock them but the produce people say there isn't much call for daikons. It's not hard to understand why! Each barrack would send someone to the kitchen to get the food, then portion it out to the prisoners. We caught one of our delivery guys keeping all the vegetables for himself, so several of us beat the shit out of him. There are always a few bad apples even among your own, but I was never aware of actual collaboration, other than Myrtle's photographer, who was not a regular member of our crew. His treachery damn near got me shot.

Surprisingly, POWs spent little time thinking of or talking about sex. When you are always hungry, sex is simply not a high priority subject. A

T-bone steak would beat it all hollow. Once in a while if rations increased a little, we might pay a bit more attention to the subject of sex.

We bedded down on straw tatami mats on wooden bunks—I won't use the word 'slept' because conditions were not conducive to sleep. Bunks were a far cry from the soft feather pillows with warm blankets and innerspring mattresses most of us used to take for granted. We had one light blanket—winter or summer. Japan's weather is about on a par with San Francisco's. In wintertime I was cold twenty-four hours a day. The lice were cold too, so every morning I would inspect seams in my clothing for them, where they would embed themselves for my body warmth. Highly prized American cigarettes became almost legal tender. Each Red Cross package contained two packs. But as I said before, the majority of these compassionate and vital gifts never reached us—they either detoured to the guards or the black market.

There was no organized political propaganda directed at us. However in one-on-one dialogue, the Nips told us that much of the territory they conquered for the "Greater East Asia Coprosperity Sphere" was historically theirs. Of course I nodded in agreement in a 'go-along to get-along' mode. They did not encourage us to learn their language. What language we did acquire visiting casually with the guards, we just picked up on our own. Unlike the POW camps in Germany, which we heard offered certain amenities, we had absolutely nothing in English to read, no games, no playing cards—nothing to help pass the time. Yankee ingenuity improvised playing cards from the bottoms of tea cartons.

However, the Japanese were sports enthusiasts and did provide baseball and softball equipment. We had two American teams. I was manager of one and a Jap guard managed the other. When my team won, the Japanese manager became furious and hit me in the mouth. As I realized that first day on the patrol boat, life here was not a two-way street. If I'd have hit him back, I'd have been a dead man. He was a bully with all the cards stacked in his favor, which, of course, is the only way bullies will play.

I don't know why the provision in the Geneva Convention against officers being forced to work was observed at Ofuna—they certainly ignored all the other humanitarian rules completely. We passed much of the time walking the perimeter of the camp and commiserating with one another. The only work I was ever required to do was carrying 'honey pots' (buckets of feces) out of the latrines for use as fertilizer. This ancient recycling practice is common in the Orient, developed over centuries to wring the highest possible return from limited land area in order to feed an ever-increasing population.

The Japanese are personally a very clean people. They believed that even prisoners should have a degree of cleanliness. We were allowed a hot bath in a community bathhouse once a week, but not without an audience. When we went in to bathe, some girls who apparently worked discreetly for the guards would make it a point to come and watch. If a guy was well endowed, they would giggle and acknowledge it, saying, "takusan, takusan!" (kind of a female wolf whistle). But if he were small, they'd smirk and say, "sukoshi, sukoshi."

As the war started going seriously against Japan in 1944, Ofuna guards beat us every time the Allies took back another Jap-held island, mostly using their fists, but when the Allies took back Tinian Island early in September, they were so mortified that they herded about thirty of us out in the yard and beat us with baseball bats. I was struck repeatedly in the kidney area and started passing blood in my urine. As a result, I had to undergo corrective surgery after the war at the Veteran's Hospital in Oakland, California. The surgery was skillfully done but the post-operative care left something to be desired. There was no recovery room so, still anesthetized, I was wheeled into my room and left with only Betty to watch me. She says there were no raised sidebars to keep me in the bed. Suddenly, without any warning, I rose up and toppled over, falling right out of bed, headfirst. Betty was horrified and got help immediately. Very fortunately, Dr. Purcell had done his work well. Not a stitch pulled loose and I seemed none the worse for wear. Everyone said afterward that was the best place for a hard head like me to land!

After nine months of starvation and beatings at Ofuna, I was just about at the end of my rope. I weighed around 105 pounds (normal weight 165) and had severe dysentery. My feet were in terrible shape from beriberi caused by a lack of Vitamin B. The word beriberi means 'I cannot' in an Asian language because the victim is too sick to do anything. Not only can it cause paralysis and pain, but muscle tissue breaks down and anemia develops. I began to have great difficulty walking and developed skin problems to boot. My kidneys were still causing problems.

We ate anything we could get our hands on. One day someone caught a skinny cat and cooked it. Tough but not too bad at that.

CHAPTER 15

OMAURI

By October 1944, I had been a "guest of the Emperor" for one year. I was in such bad shape that I was assigned to be transferred to Omauri along with some other prisoners who seemed likely to die. Omauri was a much larger camp on Tokyo Bay run by the army, and chances for medical treatment were said to be better there. (Geneva Convention beginning to have an effect?) Incurable optimist that I am, I was glad because I figured nothing could be worse than Ofuna. We were loaded on an open truck and bounced 80 painful miles over amazingly bad roads to our new location. Omauri was indeed a change for the better because the army didn't put up with guards stealing prisoner's food like they did at that Ofuna hellhole.

As a matter of fact, the move to Omauri was probably the luckiest thing that could happen to me and equally sick Tracy DuMont throughout our entire time in Japanese hands. Literally it saved my life, and not necessarily for reasons intended. Omauri was a much larger camp, housing about 800 men. The reason it was so much benefit to me was that I was assigned to a barracks with a bunch of former British convicts who stole enough food not only for themselves, but for their buddies as well. The English had been holding those guys in southeast Asia jails when the war broke out, and had given them pardons in return for joining the army to fight the Japanese. Many had been professional jewel thieves in England. They organized themselves into an *ad hoc* military unit of about 39 men and dubbed themselves "The Royal Scots." They were fierce fighters until they had to surrender at Hong Kong. As competent burglars, they were adept at stealing almost anything that wasn't nailed down. However, true to the well-known adage about 'honor among thieves,' they would never steal from a fellow prisoner.

One of my first evenings at Omauri, a Royal Scot named Fitzgerald saw me eating dinner. He said, "Lieutenant, you're in pretty bad shape. Don't eat that rice. It's two thirds barley and will make your diarrhea worse."

I feebly protested that I was starving. He said not to worry, he and his boys would feed me and take care of me. Shortly, he produced some crabmeat and sugar, an odd combination but it tasted like ambrosia to me. He also arranged to get me bismuth compound that brought a halt to the runs. I had become so weak that it took two of them just to get me up from squatting over the 'benjo' (the hole in the floor that served elimination needs). Those guys were wonderful to me and I know I would have died if it hadn't been for them. [*Editor's note: How can I ever thank them!*]

The Royal Scots managed to make off with enormous amounts of shrimp, sugar, crabmeat, and anything else edible that they could lay their hands on while working at the wharves. They did it right under the eyes of the inspectors, too. One little Irishman, Paddy, used an audacious and risky strategy to bring out a can of crabmeat. An inspector screened everyone returning from work, making us hold our hands in the air so we could be patted down. It was a fast process and the inspector always looked down, never up, so Paddy took his can of crab from his pocket and held it discretely above his head. After passing the checkpoint, it went back in his pocket. That brave and resourceful bunch sewed little pockets in the seams of their clothing to hide sugar in.

Once when we were low on sugar, Father Brown was perilously close to death from starvation—the same Father Brown who had been made to stand at attention all night long as punishment for asking to hold Sunday services for the camp. Paddy volunteered to get sugar, but since there was no sugar freighter at the dock, he had to risk going to the warehouse. He shimmied up four floors through an air duct to get it, managing somehow to escape detection, and came back with the sugar.

An amusing incident took place involving Commander Fitzgerald (no relation to the jewel thief I just told you about). He was a submarine skipper captured with his crew when their sub was forced aground. There was a feisty little Jap who liked to draw a circle on the ground and challenge anyone to step inside and take him on. None of the other Japanese liked him. He was the local bully boy. One day he taunted Fitzgerald to get in the circle with him. Fitzgerald said he'd do it if he could defend himself. The bully agreed, but what he what didn't know was that his opponent had been the boxing coach at Annapolis. Fitzgerald just beat the shit out of him, and knocked him cold, to the delight of everyone including the guards who couldn't stand him either.

With world attention now focusing on prisoners of war, the Japanese attempted to improve their image by allowing us to record a 25-word sugar-coated message that would be broadcast on Tokyo Rose's late night program, beamed not only to our troops in the South Pacific, but to shortwave receivers on the Pacific coast of the good old U.S. We didn't want to appear as though we were collaborating in a propaganda ploy, but we wanted desperately to get word to our loved ones. At the time, Betty didn't know whether I was dead or alive. We agonized over whether it would be okay to do this. Our senior prisoner officer made the decision that we should take advantage of this opportunity to get word to some of our distraught families at home. The possibility of a family receiving word that we were at least alive outweighed the possible perception that we might be helping the enemy clean up its act. I made several messages and Betty received three of them.

My first message was broadcast in October 1944, almost a year to the day after I was shot down. It was the first word Betty received that I had survived the crash of Fyrtle Myrtle and been taken prisoner. She and our young son, Bill, were asleep at her parents' home when the phone rang late one night with a long distance call from a woman in San Gabriel, California, who said, "I have a message from your husband for you." Betty damn near died. She told me that she grabbed a pencil, but after hearing the 25-word message, there was nothing on the paper but some chicken scratching. She was just numb. Within a few days she received the same message via U.S. mail from a number of other shortwave listeners along the Pacific coast.

When I got back to San Francisco after the war, Betty told me that a man by the name of B.O. South who owned a bar there had sent her a recording of the message so she was able to hear my voice. She knew then, beyond the shadow of a doubt, that I had been taken prisoner, but as to whether I was alive or not at that very moment, she still couldn't be sure. Mr. South made thousands of records and sent them to the families. When Betty mailed money to him to help with costs of recording and postage, he returned it with the explanation that since he was physically unable to be in military service, this was his contribution to the war effort. That made me extra proud to be an American. We visited him to thank him personally for all he had done.

Many other patriotic ham radio operators spent every night taking down Tokyo Rose's messages and relaying them to the families, but Mr. South was the only one who made it possible for Betty to hear my voice. These broadcasts, of course, were not meant by the Japanese to be compassionate; rather they were laced with propaganda meant to dishearten the troops such as suggesting that their wives and sweethearts had probably forgotten about them and were out playing around. However, I doubt if that weakened the resolve of even one G.I.

Lt. Colonel Jim Walker, who had become a very close friend, had not been allowed yet to send a message. I volunteered to include a word to his wife in one of mine. He gave me his wife's maiden name and her folk's address in Newport News, Virginia. My message went something like this, "Dear Betty: I'm in good health. Kiss our Bill for me. Please tell my sister, Fran Lewis (code for Jim's wife) in Newport News, Virginia (I can't remember their address but it went through okay) that Jim sends his love." That was the only word Fran ever had that Jim was alive. He eventually returned to her and their two children and spent many fruitful years working in the aerospace industry, and we saw a lot of them as, postwar, both families lived in the Denver area.

Prisoner of War Mail
~~Civilian Internee Mail~~
(Cross out one.)

POST CARD

NEW YORK, N.Y. 11:30 AM 1944

Postage Free

1ST LT. WILLIAM McFERREN
(NAME)
U.S. PRISONER OF WAR
c/o JAPANESE RED CROSS
TOKYO, JAPAN
Via New York, New York

11354
U.S. CENSOR

FORM 2277
JUNE 1944

From: BETTY G. McFERREN
P.O. BOX 266
CORONA, CALIFORNIA, U.S.A.
(FULL NAME AND ADDRESS)

NOVEMBER 6, 1944
(DATE)

DearEST SWEETIE:
YOU WILL NEVER KNOW THE THRILL IT WAS TO HEAR YOUR MESSAGE VIA TOKYO RADIO. OUR FAMILIES ARE FINE. BILL IS IN THE PINK.

I LOVE YOU —
Betty

Messages must be not more than 24 words. Type or hand print in block capitals.

Form OC-13
(Rev. June 1942)

THIS COMMUNICATION IS RETURNED TO SENDER BECAUSE IT MENTIONS:

______ DEFENSE MATTERS.

______ SHIPPING.

______ WEATHER CONDITIONS.

______ LOCATION OF U.S. FORCES.

Reference to receipt of radio broadcast is objectionable in mail destined for enemy territory.

11184
(Supervisor's No.)

1354
(Examiner's No.)

16—27982-2 GPO

SHORT WAVE LISTENING POST

G. C. GALLAGHER, 18 Delano Ave.
San Francisco, California.

Date July 10, 1945 Time 8:30 A.M.
Station JVU3 Location Tokyo, Japan Freq. 11.89 mc.
Message (Information) for you as follows:

"DEAR FOLKS: NOW YOU KNOW I AM A P.O.W. IN JAPAN. I AM IN GOOD HEALTH AND SPIRITS. ONLY WAITING FOR THE DAY WHEN I CAN BE WITH YOU AND OUR GIRL....CORONA AND SAN FRANCISCO...LOSS OF JOHN FARRINGTON AND PERRY, DE GROTE A SEVERE BLOW. NOTIFY ....56th ST., NEWPORT NEWS THAT JIM SENDS LOVE. HOPE BY THIS TIME YOU AND BILL ARE IN COOPERSTON OR CORONA. WRITE OFTEN: SEND PHOTOS. LOVE TO ALL."

Message in part as received over short wave radio from Lt. W. McFarren, U.S.A. C. now interned in P.O.W. camp at Tokyo, Japan. Address is this camp, c/o Int. Red Cross, Geneva.

Above heard by writer and relayed with best wishes. Please acknowledge. V...—

Yours truly,
G.C. Gallagher

Mrs.McFerren,

I am sending you a message I heard over short wave 7/10/45 from Japan this a.m.in case you did'nt hear it.From your husband,William,in Tokyo,#9-736015.He said,"You by this time must know that I am a prisoner in Japan. I am in good health and spirits and only waiting for the day to be with you and our own Bill.All of my thoughts are of you and our wonderful family in Corona and S.F.,give them my love.Shocked to hear about,John Farning and Ferrington.Console Betty....and Degrots. Glavin and Ben Don,were also lost,the others are all right.Notify.(I missed the name.)341, 56th St.,New Port,(sounded like"news") that Jim sends his love. Don't worry,hope you and Bill have been....or vice-versa.Love,Bill."

Sorry I missed some but hope you can make it out. Sincerely Mrs Morgan.

No.

(CENSOR'S STAMP)

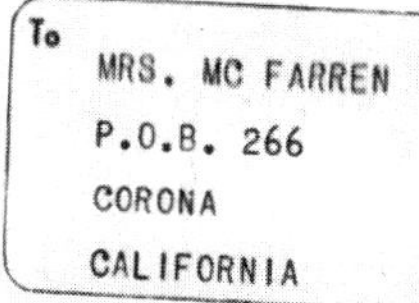

To

MRS. MC FARREN
P.O.B. 266
CORONA
CALIFORNIA

From

J. GONZALEZ RM2C
(Sender's name)

USS TRIPOLI K DIV.
(Sender's address)

%FLEET POST OFFICE

SAN FRANCISCO, CAL.
(Date)

DEAR MRS. MC FARREN,

I AM A RADIOMAN SERVING ABOARD AN AIRCRAFT CARRIER OF THE PACIFIC FLEET AND WHILE LISTENING IN ON A BROADCAST FROM RADIO TOKYO I INTERCEPTED QUITE A FEW MESSAGES FROM BOYS WHO ARE INTERNED IN THE JAPANESE HOMELAND AS PRISONERS OF WAR. NOT KNOWING WHETHER OR NOT THE GOVERNMENT NOTIFIES THE PEOPLE BACK HOME ABOUT THESE MESSAGES, I HAVE TAKEN THE LIBERTY TO DO SO IN THE HOPES THAT IT WILL THROW A BIT OF LIGHT AS TO THE WHEREABOUTS OF YOUR LOVED ONE. I SINCERELY HOPE THIS MESSAGE REACHES YOU AND BRINGS WITH IT A LITTLE RAY OF SUNSHINE YOU SO RIGHTLY DESERVE.

SINCERELY YOURS,

Julio Gonzalez

JULIO GONZALEZ RM2C
UNITED STATES NAVY

THIS MESSAGE WAS INTERCEPTED ON THE 10TH OF JULY AND CAME FROM THE PRISONER OF WAR CAMP AT TOKYO, JAPAN.

FROM: 1ST LT. W. MC FARREN ASN 0-736015

TO: MRS. MC FARREN

TEXT: NOW YOU MUST KNOW I AM A PRISONER OF WAR IN JAPAN. I AM IN GOOD HEALTH AND WAITING FOR THE DAY I CAN BE WITH YOU AND OUR GAL. MY THOUGHTS ARE WITH YOU AND MY FAMILY, CORONA, AND FRIENDS. THE LOSS OF DON AND PERRY IS A BITTER BLOW AND I KNOW YOU WILL DO YOUR BEST TO CONSOLE HER.------THE OTHER BOYS A ------ TELL ? 341 66TH STREET NEWPORT NEWS, JIM SENDS HIS LOVE. DON'T WORRY, I AM WELL. BEST TO ALL AND ALL MY LOVE TO YOU.

BILL

(DUE TO ATMOSPHEREIC CONDITONS AND SUCH I MISSED A LITTLE BIT OF THE MESSAGE BUT THE MAJORITY IS COMPLETE.)

V-MAIL

U. S. GOVERNMENT PRINTING OFFICE : 1943

My situation in prison camp had only one advantage over Betty's and that was that at any given moment, I knew I was alive—she didn't. During my first year of captivity, she had only the hope that I was in one of the five to seven parachutes reported escaping from the burning Fyrtle Myrtle. Until she received that first shortwave message, she had nothing to base her hopes on but letters from friends in the 380th relating what they knew of circumstances of our last mission. Even if lady luck had smiled on me that day, she still had no assurance that I had survived shark-infested water or rigors of prison camp. How she lived through that dreadful uncertainty, I will never fully understand. She told me that she had a very strong conviction that if I were lucky enough to be in one of those chutes, my resourcefulness and determination would somehow get me through the rest of it alive.

Betty obtained a list of home addresses for all eleven of those onboard the plane October 26, and started a round robin letter in which each family could include any late news that might come their way. An interesting sidelight (does it favor heredity of environment?) is that 100% of the crew families expressed the hope that their loved ones were alive, even though that undoubtedly meant that they were in Japanese hands. The photographer's mother (he was just along for the day, not as a regular crew member) said something like "I hope and pray that my boy will not be captured alive as a prisoner of war." Like mother like son, he was the stool pigeon that cooperated with the enemy and almost got me shot by a firing squad. If I hadn't kept my mouth shut, it could have caused the death of the 90-man crew of the submarine assigned to pick us up at the prearranged rendezvous point.

When Betty received my message, it gave her morale a giant shot in the arm. She resumed letter writing, however slim might be the chance of my receiving them. Letters to POW s were limited to 25 words. It's pretty hard for Betty or me either to even give the time of day in 25 words!

At Omauri, contrary to the Geneva Convention, officers were required to work. Once when I was on detail to dig a trench, a guard started harassing me, saying that I should shovel faster and deeper. I

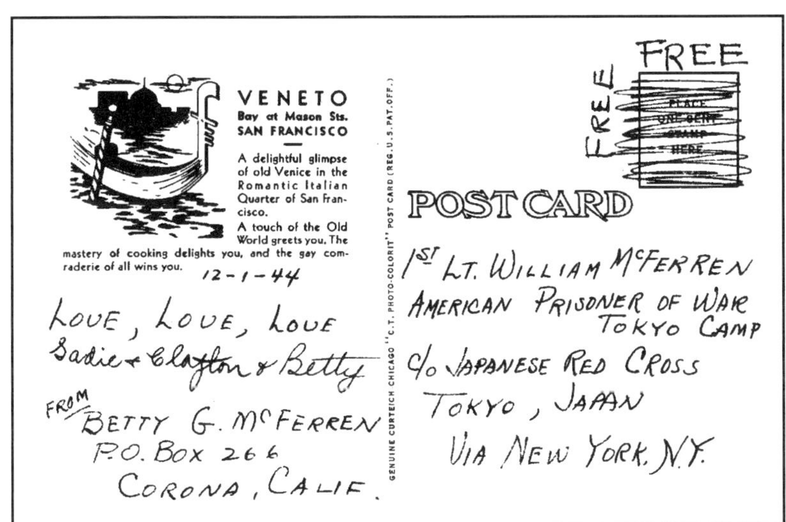

VENETO
Bay at Mason Sts.
SAN FRANCISCO

A delightful glimpse of old Venice in the Romantic Italian Quarter of San Francisco.
A touch of the Old World greets you. The mastery of cooking delights you, and the gay comraderie of all wins you.

12-1-44

Love, Love, Love
Sadie + Clayton + Betty

FROM Betty G. McFerren
P.O. Box 266
Corona, Calif.

GENUINE CURTEICH CHICAGO "C.T. PHOTO-COLORIT" POST CARD (REG. U.S. PAT. OFF.)

FREE
FREE
PLACE ONE CENT STAMP HERE

POST CARD

1st Lt. William McFerren
American Prisoner of War
Tokyo Camp
c/o Japanese Red Cross
Tokyo, Japan
Via New York, N.Y.

UNITED STATES POST OFFICE, SAN FRANCISCO 1, CALIFORNIA

PICTURE POST CARDS MAY NOT BE SENT TO A PRISONER OF WAR

Letters to prisoners of war should be placed in two envelopes The inner envelope (without postage if sent as ordinary mail and with postage affixed if sent as air mail) containing the communication properly addressed, after being sealed, should be placed in an outer envelope without postage, addressed "Postmaster-Prisoner of War Mail" and deposited in any post office, street letter box, or other authorized mail depository, or it may be handed to a clerk at a service window in any post office, or a branch or station thereof, without the outer envelope. This requirement for an outer envelope or for handing the article specially to a postal clerk is to prevent the inner letter from being postmarked with a slogan such as "Win the War", or "V" or " For Defense". Post cards and air mail letter cards for prisoners of war should be mailed in like manner. Stamps bearing like slogans should not be used. No V-Mail service is available to prisoners of war.

Prisoner of war forms bearing the endorsement "By Air Mail Par Avion" must be affixed with air mail postage at the rate of six cents for each half ounce or fraction thereof.

William H. McCarthy,
Postmaster.

WHMcC:EL:gt

told him that I was doing the best I could, so he called the camp commander, a bastard of a sergeant who hit me a couple of blows for good measure and bellowed, “I’m going to send you out for some real work,” which turned out to be another lucky break. He sent me to the nearby railroad yard with a couple of Japanese civilians to unload boxcars. One of the civilians was an older man of about 60. He poked at my shrunken stomach saying “Damae, damae,” meaning ‘very bad.’ I told him I was really hungry. After I finished my so-called lunch, he gave me a great big hot sweet potato that he had stolen and baked in the coals of the little fire we used to warm our hands. I never ate a steak in my life that tasted as good as that sweet potato. To this day, I relish sweet potatoes and yams! After I showed my appreciation to him, the old Jap and I became quite friendly and he even gave me cigarettes. Another day a truck loaded with crates of red apples was approaching. He said in Japanese, which I was beginning to understand, “Keep your eyes open.” He was trying to tell me to be alert. As the truck passed, he grabbed a crate and tossed it to me. I hid it under a tarp. When it was time to go back to camp, I was not expecting anything, but he divided those apples evenly with me. Other times we stole tuna and any other foodstuffs that were available. Slowly, I gained back 20 pounds and most of my health. I had a good relationship with the old guy and a couple others. They hated the war and the ruling military clique as much as we did. It was sort of a team effort, continually stealing small amounts of food and sharing. Sometimes, I could steal and eat enough during the day to forego the evening meal and give my food to Tracy who was still very weak.

It was hard not to become discouraged through all those months, enduring the hell of prison camp with no credible news of the battle we had left so abruptly. I felt in my heart that the U.S. would eventually win, no matter how long and how many lives that might take, but then, logically, I dared not believe that victory was assured. In war, somebody wins, but somebody always loses. What if the Allies lost? What then? I felt so alone, so abandoned, so isolated. The uncertainty was demoralizing, and the lack of news intensified it.

One day I found a Japanese dictionary in a boxcar. Not a Japanese-English dictionary, just a dictionary in one language—Japanese. I kept it, remembering that Marine Commander Harris who was an Annapolis graduate and a linguist was in our camp. I sought him out to see if he could make anything out of it. He had never studied the language, but agreed to give it a try. Sneaking as much time as he could when the Japs weren't looking, he figured out some headlines. We swiped newspapers from the guards' quarters when they were out paying obeisance to the Emperor, In about a month, Harris, who was brilliant, could pretty well scope out the war news. So now with our own private newsline, we were able to keep up a bit with things, at least from the enemy's point of view. One did, however, have to sift through a lot of propaganda to arrive at the truth. For instance, when Harris read about the Allies losing seven carriers in the Philippines and other war hyperbole, we knew when the subject was dropped that we must have taken back the Philippines. News then dealt with how many of our men and material had been captured on Okinawa. When that story appeared no longer, we correctly guessed that the Allies had retaken Okinawa. Harris was a real morale booster. Fortunately, he and his wonderful nose for news remained with us until the end of the war.

In late November 1944, after about a month at Omauri, I saw a plane the like of which I had never seen before, flying at a very high altitude over Tokyo. It was a huge four-engine aircraft—looked like a reconnaissance flight to me. Similar flights continued for several days, encouraging us since it revealed that the Allies must now have airbases closer to Japanese home soil with longer range bombers operational. We found out later those were B-29 Super-Fortresses—the biggest, longest range bombers yet built flying out of the newly conquered Mariana Islands!

A know-it-all Colonel said, "Not to worry, we won't bomb Tokyo till the Germans are out of the war." Since I had some previous experience with recces flights and follow-up bombing, I bet him a quarter of my rice ration that we would bomb Tokyo within ten days. A few days later on November 24, B-29s dumped the first bombs on Tokyo and I won the rice, a bet he didn't mind losing, even if it did cost him a couple of spoonfuls of rice: From our island prison in Tokyo Bay, we saw numerous B-29 raids and saw some of our own planes shot down; this was tough to take, but we knew that if we had new bigger bombers based close enough to bomb Tokyo, the war must be going our way.

Over the next couple of months, the bombing intensified and about mid-January 1945 carrier-based planes appeared. Camp sirens started wailing and the sky was full of Navy Hellcats. The implication was undeniable—American carriers were operating near the coast of Japan! Coincidentally, very coincidentally in fact, one of those Hellcat pilots was Bill Snyder, a Marine who was to become my business partner in Denver after the war.

Prisoners were always in danger of being hit by 'friendly fire.` We begged for paint to mark the roofs of the barracks with three letters, POW, but to no avail. Though the bombing was a real morale booster, some of the guys started to crack up under the strain—Allied pilots had no way of knowing the location of our POW camp. We could understand what the Japanese people had been going through.

One day while working in the railroad yard, I heard bombs falling and instinctively jumped behind the bank on the other side of the track, taking my two Japanese compatriots with me. The bombs hit right where we had been working.

In March 1945, Swiss Red Cross observers found out about numerous violations, including officers being forced to work at Omauri (which actually had been a blessing for me in the railroad yard). Our captors tried to evade surveillance by spreading us around to various locations, hoping to make it harder for the Red Cross to track. I was moved to a makeshift camp in a brickyard on the outskirts of Yokohama. A dramatic three months followed.

The camp commander was the biggest Japanese I had ever seen. He was 6-foot 4-inches tall and had been a hurdler in the '36 Olympics. He was a real prince and wouldn't allow his guards to hit us. This was characteristic of others who had traveled extensively outside Japan, such as the older petty officer on the boat to Singapore This big guy offered us a deal. If we planted and tended a vegetable garden, we could keep three-fourths of the crop, with the remainder going to the guards. That seemed like a fair deal, and as much as I disliked gardening, there was a real incentive here. I worked my butt off putting in a big garden on a slope behind the camp, but circumstances that developed shortly kept us from enjoying any of the fruits of our labor.

It was now May 1945. Germany had surrendered and 100% of Allied might was directed at winning the war in the Pacific. General Curtis Lemay was transferred from the European Theater to take command of the 20th Air Force, a B-29 wing in the Pacific. His strategy was saturation incendiary bombing. Our team now had the added advantage (though gained at heartbreaking cost of American life and limb) of having secured Iwo Jima in the Volcano Island chain for the Allies. This provided a desperately needed fighter base only 750 miles from the Japanese mainland. Without fighter cover, previous B-29 raids had to bomb from around 30,000 feet to avoid being intercepted by Zeros. Now with fighter cover, they could deliver much heavier bomb loads from around 6,000 feet with deadly accuracy, day or night.

May 26 proved to be a day of reckoning both for Yokohama and for our garden. Yokohama had been a beautiful modern city until bombs flattened so much of it. In the morning, a devastating air show began with what seemed like hundreds of P-51s from Iwo Jima thundering overhead. Today, they were not escorting bombers—they had come with the sole purpose of engaging Zeros in the air, and strafing those on the ground! From camp we watched a real air show over Yokohama with morbid fascination. The 51s mauled the Zeros and after finishing with them, some of our guys were so charged up and needing something else to shoot at, they made a pass over our unmarked camp. It reminded me of the sassy little flip a skillful bullfighter gives his red cape when he has vanquished the bull, turns his back, and walks away in disdain. Fortunately, by the grace of God, none of us was hit.

That evening, without Jap fighters to worry about, two waves of B-29s from Tinian Island came in low with incendiaries setting afire any of Yokahama that wasn't already burning. Right next to our camp a three-story building got hit with naphtha jelly that literally splashed all over it. The awesome power of the attack both elated and scared the hell out of me. It also destroyed part of the camp and all of our vegetable garden. The next morning, with the city still ablaze, B-29s dumped 2,000-pound delayed-action demolition bombs that ruptured water mains; thus effectively ending any fire-fighting efforts. When we lost the garden we had worked so hard on, I felt a sort of kinship with the Japanese people who were suffering so much from Allied bombs. Regardless of race, creed or color, inside our skins we're all human and have much in common. I wished that the Emperor would see the handwriting on the wall and save his people's lives and infrastructure by surrendering now—the end was clearly just a matter of time. I knew that the Japs were essentially done for, and I felt sure that if I weren't killed in the meantime, I would soon be united with Betty and Bill, my new little son.

There was an older guard in the brickyard who was decent to prisoners. He was a bit on the rotund side and we called him 'Fatty.' During one raid he was so scared he began to tremble (understandably) and simply froze. As one of the 51s came in strafing, I pushed Fatty in a slit trench and jumped in on top of him. He made a nice pillow to land on and credited me with saving his life!

I had an interesting encounter while digging one of the slit trenches. A former German officer walked by and asked me "how are they treating you?" When I told him, "Not very well," (a masterpiece of understatement) he said, "I hate to see a white man in the hands of these savages." Well, to each his own. He gave me some cigarettes and candy and told me that he had come to Japan on a ship that crossed the Indian Ocean. Don't ask me what he was doing here.

Shortly after those devastating raids on Yokohama, we were moved to Niigata, a major port city on the northwest coast of Honshu, the main island, as it was in better shape than our present surroundings were after the Yokohama bombings. Ground transportation being non-existent, we had to walk to the railroad station through the burnt out city of Yokohama. A guard told us not to smile saying, "We'll shoot anybody that smiles." There was nothing to smile about because it was truly horrible. Why wouldn't the Emperor read the tea leaves and surrender? We walked through ashes, past charred bodies and body parts—women and children—young and old—all dead and decaying. The stench was sickening, and the sight alone was enough to turn your stomach.

Footsore, we reached the railroad station and boarded a train for Niigata. Upon arrival there we were put in one of two camps that held about 500 men each. In the absence of that big strong Jap guard, we were now back to the old brutality of POW camp. Guards beat us for no apparent reason, probably their frustration over the war going against them and maybe out of fear for their own future.

One prisoner was an American doctor, Nelson Kaufman. He put out the word among the guards that if any of them got a venereal disease, he would help them. He knew they would lose pay and rank if they got caught with VD. The first night after his offer, three guards showed up. He told them the quantities of a particular medicine he needed. Within a short time they delivered all he asked for. They either had to steal it or buy it on the black market since it wasn't in the normal supply pipeline. Whatever it was, certainly it was a lifesaver against a number of other ailments as well as VD. When the wise doctor specified quantities needed, he raised the amount that was necessary far above what would cure three men and ended up with plenty to cure infections our guys had, though VD wasn't among them.

Some prisoners worked on docks, while others including myself were assigned to build air raid shelters. Allied planes gave Niigata its share of bombs, as military installations there were plentiful. Our Navy planted mines in the harbor—occasionally we saw a ship hit one. It was hard not to show our glee when that happened.

One Sunday after the war, Betty and I were watching a movie in a San Mateo, California, theater when we learned an astonishing fact. The movie was "Above and Beyond," with Robert Taylor paying the part of Colonel Tibbetts, pilot of the Enola Gay, the B-29 that dropped the first atomic bomb on Japan. The shocking fact was this: At a briefing before takeoff, three alternate targets were discussed, of which Niigata was one, but since it was weathered in, Hiroshima was designated. What an eerie 'there but for the grace of God go I' feeling! If the weather patterns had been different on August 6, 1945, I probably wouldn't be alive today to tell this tale.

The atomic bomb took its toll on our side too. Scientists had worked day and night for several years on the clandestine Manhattan Project that produced the atom bomb. It was so extremely top secret, in fact, that many who worked on it experienced severe conflict in their home lives due to strange hours and secretive behavior. Their commitment to duty strictly forbade them to discuss even one word of what was going on with anyone outside the laboratory (including spouses). Many wives became extremely suspicious and very jealous of they knew not what. Stress levels skyrocketed. I learned after the war from a friend who worked on the Manhattan Project that certain marriages went on the rocks because of the forced lack of communication.

While escape from Japan on the ground was out of the question, at Niigata three of us did consider one possibility. The camp was next to an airfield where twin engine bombers warmed up their motors near the fence. My friend, Jim Walker (whose message to his wife, Fran, I had smuggled in with my 25-word shortwave message) was a B-29 pilot. Noel Quinn, an Aussie Squadron Leader who had been shot down at Rabaul on Christmas Day, and yours truly as navigator, made up the three man crew. Quinn had hit a cable stretched across the harbor while on his way to torpedo a ship. When I heard him bitching about it for the umteenth time, I joked,"Why are you bitching, Noel, the Nips sent you a cable for Christmas!"

Our escape plan involved jumping the unguarded fence and stealing one of the bombers. Usually those planes were warmed up by a single unarmed mechanic. We figured if we timed it right, we could scramble to the plane and overpower him. As navigator, I had a crude map with a flight plan to Russia sewed in my pants. Fortunately we didn't have to use this scenario as the war ended only a couple of weeks after we started to seriously plan our escape.

CHAPTER 16

FREE AT LAST

Early one morning late in August, six Navy fighters flew over our Niigata camp at about 500 feet. No guns fired on them, nor did they strafe. Such a thing had never happened before. I hardly dared hope that today might be the day we had dreamed of for so long but feared we would never live to see. A couple of hours later, I was playing cards in the barracks with an improvised tea carton deck when I heard guys outside screaming, "Here they come! Here they come!" I dashed outside to see what was coming. It was a perfect formation of American fighters roaring down over the camp. Drawing closer, they peeled off one by one, doing victory rolls. There wasn't a dry eye among us. It was the sweetest thing we could ever hope to see! I silently gave thanks to the many whose lives had been lost to make this moment possible. Everyone knew then the war was over.

The camp commander called all officer POWs together and asked, "What is atom bomb?" We told him we didn't know, which was the truth. I felt sure that something pretty big had happened because of the letup in bombing. Several days before, on August 6 when the first atom bomb was dropped on Hiroshima and the expected surrender did not materialize, the Allies were faced with a dreadful dilemma. Japan was warned that we had a second bomb, and would use it if we had to. After the devastation wrought by the first atom bomb, and with threat of a second, how could sane persons ignore such a warning? Still there was no answer from Japan.

To bomb or not to bomb? Such are the wrenching decisions top military men must make. Invasion would be ordered if absolutely necessary, but after the agony our forces had been through and the losses

Niigata POW camp. Left to right: a guard, Bill McFerren, two unidentified prisoners, Nelson Kaufman, M.D., Ameil Palermo, M.D.
(Note body language between Bill and the guard. This was probably at the war's end - exact date unknown.)

Supplies and mud at Yonton Strip on Okinawa shortly before the surrender.

DENVER POST 11-4-03

Smithsonian bombs again

When it comes to the Enola Gay, the Boeing B-29 bomber that dropped an atomic bomb on Hiroshima, Japan, on Aug. 6, 1945, the Smithsonian Institution seems able to do no right.

In 1994, the museum enraged World War II veterans with a display that implied the United States has unjustly committed aggression against Japan.

In August, the reassembled Enola Gay, named for command pilot Col. Paul Tibbets Jr.'s mother, was put on display near Dulles International Airport outside Washington, D.C. This time, criticism came from scholars, writers and antiwar activists angered that the exhibit focuses on the B-29's technological advances rather than its role in dropping the first atomic weapon ever used in war.

That criticism is valid: Of 4,000 B-29s built during World War II, the only reason the Smithsonian has the Enola Gay is that it *was* the Hiroshima plane. Ignoring that fact is a little like focusing on the Titanic's superior engineering and not mentioning the iceberg.

The story of the Enola Gay has fallen victim to some severe historical revisionism. At the time of the 1994-95 controversy, one of the "facts" that angered veterans groups was an estimate of 30,000 to 50,000 American combat deaths predicted for a full-scale invasion of Japan. A "compromise" put the figure at 1 million, which was denounced as "historical cleansing" by those holding opposing views.

President Harry S. Truman, who gave the OK to using the atomic bombs, had been told by his top military advisers that an American invasion of the Japanese home islands might cost 500,000 American lives and possibly more than 1 million Japanese deaths.

Latter-day historians who challenge those figures ignore the fact that Imperial Japan held about 300,000 Westerners (civilian and military) as slave laborers and had vowed to execute all of them if the home islands were invaded.

Also, Japan — unlike its defeated Axis ally, Germany — still had about 2 million troops under arms, not a small thing considering the bloody campaigns to capture Japanese-held Pacific islands such as Iwo Jima and Okinawa earlier in 1945.

President Truman made his decision in hopes that Japan would eschew its rigid no-surrender ethos once it saw the awesome power of the atom bomb. Indeed, after the first bomb was dropped, Japan's military leaders balked until Emperor Hirohito's ordered surrender after Nagasaki was bombed.

We also note that the Hiroshima death toll seems to have experienced some inflation over the years: One reporter writing about the current Enola Gay exhibit said 140,000 were killed instantly and 230,000 in all, including radiation victims. That compares with wartime estimates of 60,000 to 100,000 deaths in the initial blast.

Point is, the lessons of that tragic era are too important to allow the facts to be distorted for any purpose — either by the Smithsonian or anybody else.

sustained to bring us to this point—bloody naval battles—the Coral Sea, a four-day marathon fought in a hurricane, Leyte Gulf. the decisive costly Battle of Midway among them, as well as the many landings on fiercely defended Japanese-held islands that lay behind on beaches of Tarawa, Kwajelein, Bouganville, and many others including one of the last and bloodiest, Iwo Jima, memorialized by the magnificent bronze statue in Arlington Cemetery of three Marines raising the Stars and Stripes in triumph atop Mt. Surabachi—how could we ask our forces for even more? Many thousands of dead and maimed lay in the wake of those battles so far from our country's shores and so terribly critical to America's survival.

The War Department just couldn't ask one more serviceman to lay down his life in an invasion when we held the ace card in our arsenal. If the Japanese war machine insisted on following the dictates of their man-god, Hirohito,who knew more about Shintoism than he did about military strategy, then it had to be their funeral, even though it was a death sentence for thousands of people—men, women and children, military and civilian.

Three days later, the second bomb was dropped. Our military was not aware of it, but we prisoners had been told that if there were an invasion, all POWs would be shot.

After that second bomb on Nagasaki, even the Japanese had to admit defeat. The following day they asked that peace negotiations might begin; first though, inquiring if "unconditional surrender" meant that Emperor Hirohito would have to give up his throne. To me he was a mass murderer but the ancestor worship of the Japanese people paid him blind obeisance. The Allied reply stated that this was something the Japanese people would have to decide for themselves, but otherwise, surrender would <u>have</u> to be completely, unconditionally UNCONDITIONAL.

The sudden end of hostilities took us and the Japanese people by complete surprise. Sometimes it had seemed that the war would never end and that we were destined to live out what was left of our lives in this filthy, rat-infested place under jurisdiction of these unpredictable, half-insane despots. Our newsman, Commander Harris, had not foreseen an imminent end to hostilities because it was not reported in newspapers, which, of course, sugar-coated everything. The elite must have understood only too well the hopeless situation they were in, but either through denial or vain hope, chose to hide it from the public as long as possible.

Postwar analysis showed that from mid-1945, American submarines, aircraft and surface vessels had blockaded practically all imports of war materials so the home islands were virtually cut off from any source of supply. The ruling clique could not help but realize the impossibility they were facing. Knowing this, it seems to me that it was unconscionable for them to allow one more life, theirs or ours, to be sacrificed down that deadend road to nowhere.

Now that the war's end was taking shape, we were in a kind of limbo—the guards knew better than to abuse us, while we didn't know what to expect or what to do next. The Camp Commander asked us if we wanted the guards pulled out of camp. We called a hasty POW meeting and agreed that, yes, we did want them out of the barracks, but not out of camp as we feared wrath from local citizens.

This concern, however, proved to be unfounded. From working with the old Jap in the railroad yard where we stole food together, I had learned that there were different degrees of militarism among civilians. By no means were all of them gung-ho for the war. This was shown in the opening scenes of "Tora! Tora! Tora!" a really great, authentic movie about Pearl Harbor. It showed the high command of Nipon discussing whether or not to make war on the United States. The young aggressive officers were all for it while an older one warned, prophetically, "We will awaken a sleeping giant."

Finally we got the buckets of yellow paint we had needed for so long in order to mark the roofs of the barracks with big letters: POW. Actually, this was not through altruism on the part of our captors—they had orders from Allied Headquarters to identify where food drops should be made. During the next few days planes dropped not only food but newspapers, medical supplies, etc. What a field day we were having! A vicious guard, hated by the prisoners and other guards alike, was standing in the yard and I saw a box falling straight toward him. He started to walk out of the way so I called to him. He stopped just long enough to get clobbered by the box! Sweet revenge.

My buddy, John Lardin, Myrtle's Flight Engineer, got quite a thrill when he opened one of the air drops. There was a note inside that read, "Greetings from Ed Falenski, Natrona, Pennsylvania." Believe it or not, John was from Natrona and had known Ed when they were both civilians there. He planned to look up Ed when he got home.

A prisoner I knew by the name of Faulkner learned about the end of hostilities in a rather unusual way. He was interned in a Manchurian prison camp when he heard voices in the next room. He thought his ears were playing tricks on him because it sounded like English was being spoken. He climbed up on a desk to peek through a crack between the wall and the ceiling. He could hardly believe what he saw: An American officer with his feet on a desk, smoking a big cigar! He raced to tell his buddies who slipped in silently one by one to squeeze their heads against the ceiling and peer through that crack. They all felt like whooping and hollering, but with the ingrained caution learned from months of abuse, kept quiet for the moment, anyway.

They all knew then, of course, that the war was over, but since they were so far from the Japanese home islands, they did not expect immediate rescue, so Faulkner and a buddy took off walking through the countryside hoping for kindness from the people to keep them alive till they reached friendly territory. Amazingly, this was no problem as they were well treated by the farmers, confirming my conviction that all nationalities would have so much in common inside their skins if they weren't brainwashed by self-serving factions.

Now adhering to rules of the Geneva Convention, the Japanese paid us what we were supposed to get in yen. I forget exactly what that sum was but anyway I won a lot more in a poker game so I had around 30,000 yen. I bought a cow and two goats from a farmer for 3,000 yen.

Example of money paid to us at the war's end

One of our boys had worked for the Armour packing plant before the war, so he was appointed official butcher. The meat was simmered all day and what a feast we had! A filet at the Waldorf couldn't have tasted better! Nobody got sick even though we were all guilty of overeating.

On September 1, the day before the official surrender on the USS Missouri, a bunch of us visited what was left of the city. It felt like a surrealistic dream to be walking down the streets of Niigata in broad daylight, destruction on all sides, Japanese lettering on signs everywhere, not a word written or spoken in English, and yet we felt safe. After our years of abuse by their military, civilians smiled and treated us with courtesy. Were we dreaming? Were we actually alive? Our world had done a complete 180 degree turnaround taking us with it, and we were welcome to enjoy the pleasures of what had once been a beautiful, bustling city. Our bombs had not completely disrupted utilities or the flow of life in Niigata, since many places were conducting business as usual!

Many younger people today, who have probably never been shot at or bombed, feel that atom bombs were a case of overkill. They claim that the same results could have been achieved more humanely or 'diplomatically,' as evidenced by the furor over the wording of the Enola Gay exhibit at the Smithsonian. That position probably springs from humanitarian impulses, but they may not be aware of what history tells us about the conclusion of the first World War. Sumner Wells, President Franklin Roosevelt's Under Secretary of State in his book, *The Time for Decision*, written in 1944, describes how inept was the handling of negotiations in 1918 when that Armistice was signed. Webster's Dictionary defines the word "armistice" as "a brief cessation of arms by convention; a temporary cessation of hostilities," and that is exactly what that war's end turned out to be—brief and temporary. Another far bloodier and more costly conflict erupted when Hitler kicked off World War II by invading Poland in 1939, only twenty-one years after that inept 1918 Armistice was signed.

Welles says, "It is, of course, well known that up to the last moment, Allied leaders assembled in Paris were not sure whether the German representatives would actually sign the treaty of Versailles or not." David Lloyd George, the British Prime Minister, was even concerned during the final stages of the conference that many terms, already agreed upon, would have to be modified to obtain German signatures!

"In practice, the Treaty proved to be neither a negotiated peace, nor peace by imposition." Wells continues, revealing things hitherto unknown to many who may not be students of history. "At the time of the Armistice, Germany had not been invaded by Allied Forces. So far as the masses of German people could see, the collapse of Germany and her decision to sue for an Armistice had been due to the breakdown of organized resistance within Germany, rather than to military defeat." The Allies had failed to be tough enough in 1918 to impose terms of unconditional surrender upon Germany.

CHAPTER 17

THE GOLDEN GATE

After the surrender, numerous conferences and much planning had to be hastily pulled together. U.S. authorities requested that the Japanese send their top officer from each camp to assist in arranging prisoner evacuation. One of our ranking American officers, Major Fellows, went to Yokohama accompanied by a Japanese officer. They boarded Admiral Halsey's flagship to plan repatriation details. I heard a funny story about something that happened on the ship's quarterdeck. Fellows turned to a Navy Chief and nodding toward the Japanese officer, said "Take care of this guy." The Chief, misunderstanding pulled out his gun, thinking Fellows meant to shoot the officer. The Major hastened to explain to the Chief that he had misunderstood. What he meant was, "Please see that he is made comfortable."

Admiral Halsey ordered Commander Harold Stassen, one of his aides (and later, a perennial presidential candidate) to follow up with our evacuation. The next day, Stassen flew up to Niigata, landing at the very field where only a few weeks before, Walker, Quinn, and I had made plans to steal a plane and escape. I remember Stassen arriving in camp in a Japanese truck and standing on the bed of the truck to speak to us. Everyone was standing around waiting for something to happen. He said, "Boys, I came to get you out." Loud cheers erupted. "We planned on evacuating you by sea, but since trains are running, we're sending you down to the embarkation point by rail."

Stassen summoned the Niigata Mayor and told him that he needed enough railcars to move 1,000 men, and he needed them within two days. The Mayor politely told him that such an order would be impossible, that it would take at least ten days. Stassen told the interpreter to explain to the mayor that he had to have the cars right away and if they weren't available in two days, he would order an atom bomb dropped on Niigata, which, of course, was pure BS as Stassen didn't have that authority, and wouldn't consider such a thing if he did, but the bluff worked. The Mayor was shaking in his boots and the railcars arrived on time.

On the train to Yokohama, I was heard to brag that I was going to kiss the first American woman that I laid eyes on. When we arrived, passing through the station we were met by a WAC Major. My buddy said, "O.K., McFerren, put up or shut up." So, I grabbed her and planted a big kiss on her cheek. Startled, she pushed me away in shock. Since she outranked me, I hastily explained and apologized for my behavior, and was very sweetly forgiven.

We were immediately transferred to a hospital ship for a medical checkup. If the exam showed that you were able to walk, talk or otherwise exhibit signs of life, you would be flown to the island of Okinawa. When I arrived there, a Red Cross official asked, "Is there anybody on this island that you would like to contact?" Hell, I didn't know anyone remotely connected with Okinawa, so I thanked him and added casually, "I was with the 380th Bomb Group when I was shot down."

While enjoying some really good food in the mess hall, even better than that goat and beef stew in Niigata, a Red Cross worker rushed up to me and said, "Believe it or not, Lieutenant, your old bomb Group is only 14 miles from here!" I couldn't believe it! The good old 380th not only bombed me but now followed me. During my two years as a prisoner, the 380th had pushed steadily north from Australia, through the Philippines, ever closer to the Japanese Islands.

My heart was pounding—so much was happening so fast. I arranged for a car and driver to take me to Group Headquarters. At 125 pounds, I was a lot thinner than when my nickname was Porky on that one-way trip to the Celebes. None of the old timers recognized me. Finally, when they realized that it was me, it seemed to them that I had returned from the Great Beyond. (I sort of had.) After an ecstatic reunion, I searched out the Group clerk and asked a practical question: "What did you do about my promotion?" My upgrade to Captain was due only a few days after we went in the drink. Embarrassed, he answered, "I hate to tell you, but nothing was done about it."

"Damn," was all I said, thinking of the thousands of bucks that error cost me.

The 380th flew lots of released POWs to the Philippines. I flew to Manila in one of my old outfit's B-24s. It hadn't changed a bit, still as uncomfortable as ever, but a wonderful, thrilling flight for me. I still had my dog tags but for some unknown reason, I couldn't get identified and couldn't get paid. I even had to borrow $20 from the Red Cross to send a telegram to Betty to tell her I was alive!

I remember hanging around Manila for about a week, growing angrier by the day. I began to think MacArthur's people didn't give a damn about the Air Corps. It seemed to me they were only processing those captured in the Philippines. Finally, I got really pissed and, fortified by three martinis, went down to the nearest motorpool and asked the Master Sergeant, "Who's the ranking American officer around here?" He told me that it was General Kenney. I asked where I might find the General.

"Probably down at Clark Field." was his laconic reply.

I explained to him, "I flew under General Kenney. He was head of the Fifth Air Force. Can I get a car and driver and go over and tell him how some of his former POW airmen are being treated?"

"Lieutenant, you will have a car in one minute," he told me, and left on the double.

We quickly covered the 40 miles to Clark Field and pulled up at General Kenney's temporary headquarters, consisting of a big tent with his four star insignia on the door. I knocked, entered, and was met by the General's aide, a WAC Major.

"Lieutenant, what's your business here?" she asked, rather crisply.

Bristling, I said, "I came over to see General Kenney."

"That's impossible" said she in her best mother tigress manner. "He's busy. He just got back from a trip. Why don't you come back in a day or two." That last was a statement, not a question.

I exploded with martini courage. "Bullshit! I want to see him right now. I flew for him. He sent me to Balikpapan twice," I was screaming, "I want to see him RIGHT now!"

Suddenly an inner door flew open and out came a couple of aides followed by the General himself. He asked, "What's going on here?" He had heard the commotion behind his closed door.

"General Kenney, Sir," I replied, "I flew with the 380th out of Manbaloo. We volunteered for the first two missions to Balikpapan. I went on to tell him what was happening to me or, more precisely, what was not happening to me.

"All MacArthur's people seem to care about are the guys captured on Bataan and Corrigedor," I told him. "I feel sorry for them but I want to go home too. I can't get identified or paid. I've been here a week! I had to borrow $20 from the Red Cross to send a wire home!"

He had a fit when he heard my story. He grabbed a phone and spent about half an hour talking very heatedly to several people. Among other profanities, I heard him say, "A lot of our boys are being shit on." Then he turned to me and said, "Can I offer you a drink?"

One of his aides had already brought out a bottle of scotch. He poured me a couple of snorts, then directed his aide to take me to the mess tent for some food and coffee. Since I hadn't had any alcohol for two years, I was completely out of training. The consensus seemed to be that I needed to sober up. Before I left, however, the General told me, "I have arranged with the Navy to take you and your group to San Francisco," words that not too long before would have seemed about as far-fetched as a promised trip to the moon. He went on to say, "You will sail at 16:30 hours tomorrow. I'm sending you guys directly home and you will have nurses to look after you."

When I got back to Manila, a Colonel called me in to his office and asked if I were the guy that had just been talking to General Kenney's Headquarters. I told him I was his man.

He was irate. "You got me in a lot of trouble," he snapped, "Now I have to call Headquarters every hour and report the name of every Air

Corps ex-POW that passes through here."

"Tough shit." I thought, but managed to keep my mouth shut, which is somewhat unusual for me.

General Kenney also arranged for immediate advances against back pay owed to us. In my case, that was only about $4,000 as I had directed a generous allotment on a monthly basis to Betty and the baby. She saved most of it, living at home with her parents and had invested some of it in San Clemente real estate. I drew $500 and lent $300 to a fellow POW from Niigata, a Norwegian ship captain named Carlson who needed it to get home. Later Betty asked me how I could be so sure he would pay me back. Under the circumstances we were in, you learn very quickly, almost with animal-like instinct, to size people up correctly. His check arrived two weeks after I was back in the States.

When I sent Betty a cable telling her the date and time I would arrive in San Francisco on the SS Yarmouth, it gave me a very strange feeling after dealing with tough censorship restrictions in my letters from Australia and Japan—information like that had been strictly verboten and I even had to talk in code about "my friend Myrtle, "being on a trip" and "business being brisk today." No information was classified now and I was free to say anything that came into my head. It still seemed very strange.

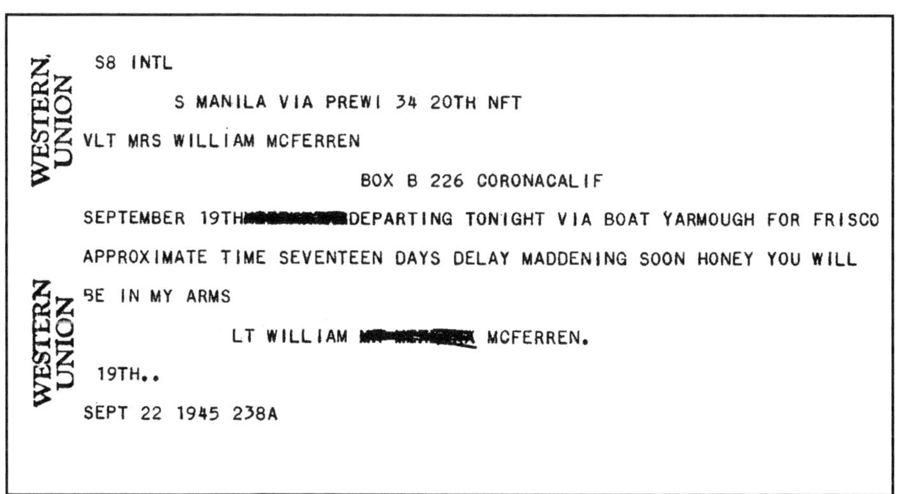
WESTERN UNION

S8 INTL

S MANILA VIA PREWI 34 20TH NFT

VLT MRS WILLIAM MCFERREN

BOX B 226 CORONACALIF

SEPTEMBER 19TH DEPARTING TONIGHT VIA BOAT YARMOUGH FOR FRISCO APPROXIMATE TIME SEVENTEEN DAYS DELAY MADDENING SOON HONEY YOU WILL BE IN MY ARMS

LT WILLIAM MCFERREN.

19TH..

SEPT 22 1945 238A

As scheduled, the Yarmouth sailed the next afternoon and during the two and a half week voyage, I gained 25 pounds! Thankfully, it was daylight when we passed under the Golden Gate Bridge, and just about everyone was on deck to savor the moment and give silent thanks to our country for what it had done. I felt like my chest was going to explode. I don't think there were many dry eyes among us.

After the Yarmouth tied up to the San Francisco pier, for some strange reason we could not come ashore for two hours. Of course all passengers crowded the rail searching faces on the dock for their loved ones. I quickly spotted Betty wearing a white feather hat on her dark brown hair. Whether clothes, perfume or feathers, she always had a flair for attracting attention. Her aunt and uncle, Sadie and Clayton Garvey, who had been like parents to us were with her. We smiled, waved and generally acted like village idiots for an awkward eternity. Eventually the gangplank dropped and I was able at last to leave the ship and hold Betty in my arms. It was unreal. We had not spoken a word nor touched one another since that day two and a half long years

The Yarmouth (looking pretty seedy but what a Godsend!) approaches the dock in San Francisco Bay.

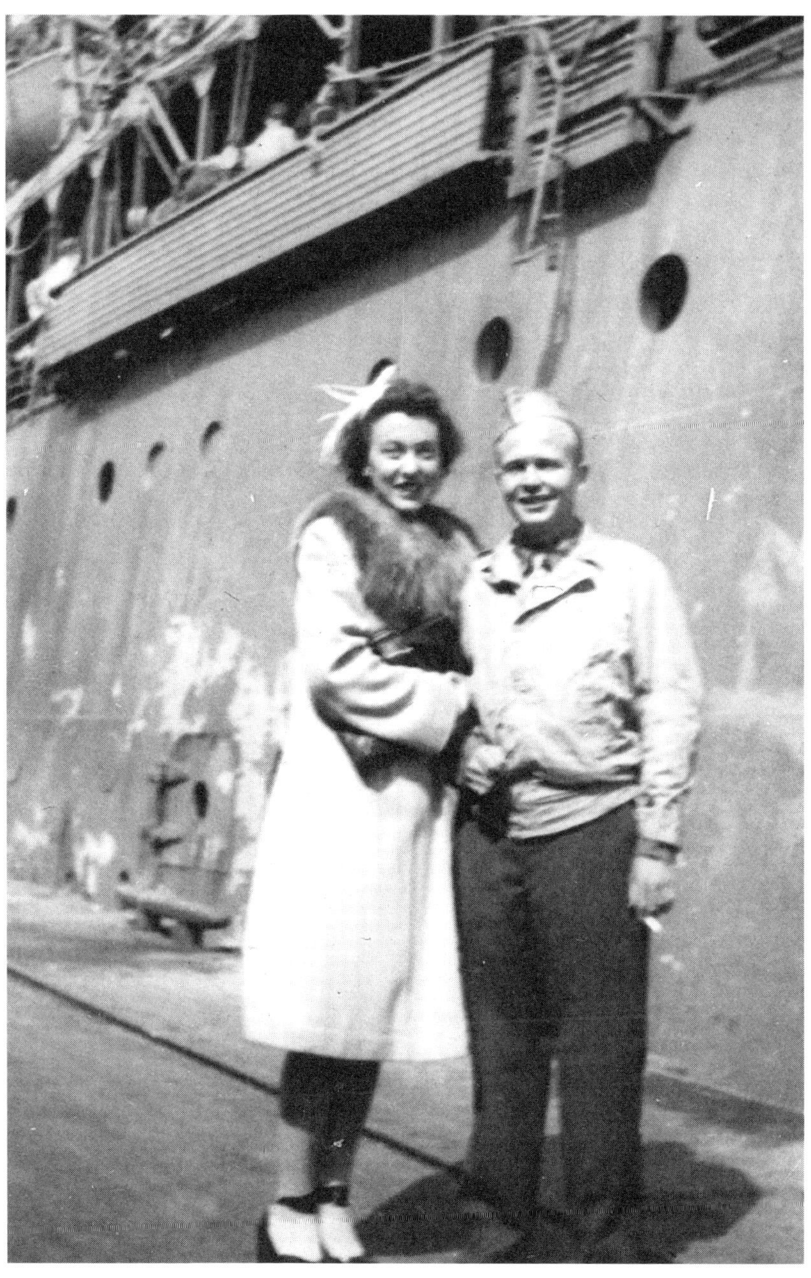

First time we'd touched each other in two and a half years!

before when we said goodbye on the corner of Sloat Boulevard and 19th Avenue. I'm not sure I could have gotten on that bus to cross the Golden Gate to Hamilton Field had I known what lay ahead in the ensuing two and a half years.

Our son Bill, now two and a half years old, was not at the pier that day. Betty had left him in the care of Louise Farnum in Santa Ana. Louise, with her sly sense of humor, had nicknamed him Duke because of the way he attacked the piano keys when they played together "I'd hate to lose you, 'cause I'm so used to you now."

Clayton and Sadie took Betty and me out to their house on Head Street. Once there, they said they had some errands to run and would be back in a few hours. Heaven! It was hard to believe I wasn't dreaming as I had done so many nights in prison camp only to awaken to reality on a cold straw mat.

The next day I reported to the Veteran's Hospital for a thorough checkup, which amazingly I passed with the exception of some overdue dental work as a result of malnutrition. Then I called Cush Farnum who now was CO of the Santa Ana Army Air Base where I had begun Air Force training, advising him of my good fortune in receiving orders to report there. I always suspected that he had had something to do with those orders.

Upon arriving at Louise's house in Santa Ana, I finally laid eyes on my son, Bill. He seemed awfully big! And he, on the other hand, didn't quite know what to make of his new Daddy. He was a very handsome child. We had a lot of catching up to do!

As soon as I could, I wrote letters to the families of the boys lost on Myrtle's last mission. After two years, some of them still had no idea what had happened to their loved ones.

After I had been back a little over a month, I decided to have some fun with Al. On October 26, he and Mickey were home in Minneapolis with his family. When our crew had left on that ill-fated mission to Pomelaa two years before (the first one without him), he told me he'd meet me at the flightline when we got back and, of course, was dreadfully apprehensive when we did not show up. So, exactly two years later to the day, hour, and almost to the minute at 6 o'clock, I called Al (who in the hustle and bustle of post-war commotion hadn't learned that I was alive and back on U.S. soil).

When he answered the phone, I said, "Paris, this is Porky. We're back. Come pick me up."

POSTSCRIPT

Following the war, Bill was West Coast Sales Manager for Uncle Ben's Rice. When offered the job, he bought a package of the product, cooked up a cupful and convinced of its merits, took the job. Answering a question on the application, "What previous experience have you had with this product?", he wrote "I ate rice as a POW in Japan for two years."

After seven years with Uncle Ben's, he went in the food brokerage business with Bill Snyder, one of the Marine pilots who dropped food to the prisoners when the war ended. Bill fished, worked in Republican politics, played golf and rode horseback with Betty and retired from the brokerage business in 1977.

APPENDIX

Even though things at Fenton Field seemed pretty primitive, the two volume book written by my classmate, John W. (Jack) Field, *Rendezvous with Destiny*, published by Phoenix Publishing, Canaan, NH in 1984, reveals an even grimmer picture of the war in 1942 fought by the Air Corps in Australia, and the devastatingly bloody battles seen by the Navy and Marines, both in the air and on the beaches. Indescribable bravery and loss of life in this fight for our nation's survival – yes, I said *survival,* must never be forgotten. We must never allow future generations to become complacent. The path to peace lies through strength. I only hope that our children and our children's children will not lose their lives because their nation fell asleep at the switch, or was afraid to stand up for what they knew was right.

Following are excerpts from Jack's book which describe graphically the agony of early days in the Pacific and battles fought by Yale men. In the light of today's pinpoint bombing and low war casualties, it's important that following generations be aware of the casualties that our nation willingly sustained in the pursuit of peace.

Chapter 4, pages 54 through 73

THE JAPANESE ARE STOPPED

Futility in the Southwest, Coral Sea, Midway, Torpedo Squadron Eight, The Sinking o f the Yorktown, Guadalcanal

The first few months of 1942 were bitter indeed for the U.S. and Allied forces in the Pacific. Defeat followed defeat. With much of the American fleet destroyed at Pearl Harbor and the U.S. and Filipino troops holed up on Bataan, the Japanese moved swiftly down the Malay Peninsula to capture the great English base of Singapore. They were in New Guinea and New Britain, building a mammoth base at Rabaul; most important, they were threatening the Allied routes and lifelines to the continent of Australia. In four short months they had conquered most of Southeast Asia.

(text omitted)

1942

From early January until April 1 Ed's group flew out of Davao and out of Java, doing the little they could to stop the southern advance of the Japanese. Ed reported: "It was pathetic. We had nothing. We tried to raid their shipping, but we had no fighters for protection (all the time I was there I never saw a friendly fighter), and only a very few Flying Fortresses. I flew thirty-four missions, sixteen in seventeen days, against the Japs in Macassar Strait, and on fully half the missions ours was the only plane. At other times we had at most two to four planes. We kept trying to tell ourselves that we were doing all right, that we were hurting the Japs, but we knew we weren't even slowing them up.

"We had no command, no headquarters. We were on our own; everything started and stopped on the airfield where we were. We made up our own missions. We had no mechanics or support crews. We had to try to patch up our own planes; the flight crew themselves had to fuel them. The B-17 held 1,700 gallons of gas, and we had to load it up by hand from 5-gallon tin cans. You can imagine how long that took. We were a motley crew, just lost souls. We didn't even have uniforms. What we wore was part United States, part Dutch, part RAF. We were not even paid; forced to scrounge off the land and from people we met. I myself did not get a cent of pay from December until May."

Ed's group was finally forced to pull out of Java when the Japanese captured it. "We tried to stop their armada but it was hopeless. I watched it from 20,000 feet up and could not see the end of it, ship after ship after ship. Those of us who were lucky enough to get on a plane flew back to Australia. Many of the rest tried to escape from Java by boat, but most of them were sunk and killed by Jap submarines."

When the group left Australia for home some months later, 86 percent of the original men in it were dead.

The Americans had one big advantage: they had broken the Japanese code. With this knowledge they were privy to the enemy's strategic plan of first taking Port Moresby, thus opening up the whole northern Australian coast, and then with a mammoth naval armada, capturing Midway Island and luring the remaining American fleet units, including the carriers, into battle, when presumably they would be destroyed. With Port Moresby (and the nearby Solomon Islands) in their hands plus Midway, Japan would have cut the supply lines between the United States and Australia, achieved naval and air control over the whole Pacific Ocean, rendered Hawaii useless, and be threatening the U.S. West Coast. Under those conditions, the Japanese believed, the United States would sue for peace.

Key to the achievement of this plan was Midway. In early June the Japanese struck with a mammoth fleet of carriers, battleships, submarines, cruisers, and destroyers. The Americans, badly outnumbered, were this time ready for them.

Action began in the early morning of June 4. It was 4:30 A.M. when the first of 128 planes took off from the Japanese carrier Akagi bound for Midway. They were the same planes and same pilots that had attacked Pearl Harbor, but Midway had been warned and was armed and ready for them. Shortly after dawn an American Catalina PBY, flying reconnaissance, saw the Midway-bound planes and radioed their bearings.

(text omitted)

Fred Mears came from a family of warriors. His grandfather fought in the Spanish-American War; his father received the Distinguished Service Medal in World War I; his uncle was Lt. Gen. Jonathan M. Wainwright, who had been captured by the Japanese when, a month before Midway, the Japanese had taken Corregidor after the fall of Manila. Fred Mears was a law student and newspaper reporter before entering the navy as an aviation cadet in January *1941*. In the late spring of *1942* he boarded the *Hornet* as a spare pilot for Torpedo Squadron Eight. Of his experiences at Midway and Guadalcanal he wrote a book, *Carrier Combat*, published after his death, and from which these quotations are taken.

(text omitted)

Let Fred Mears tell the story:

"Torpedo Squadron Eight was in the ready room of the *Hornet* at about 3:30 A.M. the morning of June 4.... Suddenly the battle started for Torpedo Eight. The following message flashed on the teletype screen Many enemy planes headed for Midway.'... Over the loudspeaker came the order, 'The enemy main body is now attempting to take Midway. We are heading toward Midway to intercept and destroy them ... we intend to launch planes at 0900 to attack enemy while their planes are returning from Midway. We will close to about 100 miles of enemy position. Each group attack one carrier.'

"Our skipper, Commander Waldron, gave his pilots their last-minute instructions. 'I have no doubt we'll all be back here by noon. But if worse comes to worst and we find ourselves alone and outnumbered by enemy planes on the way in to attack, we'll keep boring in toward the carrier. And if there is only one man left I want that man to take his pickle in and get a hit!'

"'Man all planes,' the final order had come. All pilots hurriedly finished their navigation and clambered one by one out of the ready room.

"I was to go on the third attack."

"But there was no third attack. There wasn't a second attack either. In fact, we never saw any of the planes again after they left the deck."

On his way home to Pearl Harbor, Fred had the duty of inventorying the effects of the fourteen fliers and fifteen radiomen of Torpedo Squadron Eight who had not returned from their first–and only–mission. "Going through every person's private effects –seeing a characteristically battered cap, a girl's picture, an earmarked prayer book, or a wallet with various cards–made me realize how much each one would be missed at home. I also had to skim through the letters each had received before we sent them back to the nearest of kin, and in them we saw expressed the love and good luck wishes that seemed so futile now. Many of the officers and men had written last-minute notes, as Waldron had advised, and in censoring these ... I found the last heartfelt thoughts of brave men."

The only survivor of the men who took off that morning from the *Hornet* was a friend of Fred's, Lt. Tex Gay. The other part of Torpedo Eight (the planes flown directly to Midway and launched from there) had suffered a similar fate. Only one plane, piloted by Lt. Bert Earnest, with a dead gunner and a wounded radioman, returned to Midway. A couple of weeks later Fred Mears saw both of these fliers in Hawaii. From them he heard the story:

"The last and only attack by Torpedo Eight took place just about as Waldron hoped it wouldn't. When he didn't find the Jap force where contact reports had placed it, he played his hunch, turned westward, and flew until the squadron stumbled on the track of the enemy.

"He found the Jap carriers, first sighting them by smoke smudges on the horizon. He made his contact report, thus revealing the exact position of the Jap striking force to our carrier squadron for the first time since early morning. Waldron's main contribution to the course of the battle was, in fact, locating the enemy fleet, not in his do-or-die attack, glorious as that was.

"After sighting the enemy fleet, he put his nose down, leveled off just above the water and went on in. Behind him as he closed toward a volume of Jap A.A. fire were the faithful pilots of his squadron. Behind them... were carrier-based Zeros doing wing-overs and half loops at 250 knots to get into firing position on the tails of the flying freight cars bearing the white star. One by one, our TBD's, poking along at 120 knots, crashed into the sea under fire from the Zeros' deadly 20-millimeter cannons. The skipper went down in flames. Finally there was only one plane left.

" 'And if this happens I want that pilot to take his pickle in and get a hit.'

"Tex Gay probably wasn't thinking of Waldron's exact words as he skimmed over the water on that last mile, A.A. raking the sea in front of him, the yellow lines of tracer fire streaking past his wings and the bulk of one of the biggest Jap carriers looming in front of him. But unconsciously, because of his training under the skipper and because he was from Texas, this last pilot of Torpedo Eight did just that. Then he flipped his plane over the bow of the carrier, shot down at last. A few moments later he heard an explosion. It was his torpedo going home. "Gay stayed afloat in his Mae West jacket until sundown and then inflated his rubber boat and clambered in. What he saw that day was the successful follow-up of Waldron's suicidal attack. Tex watched as American dive-bombers, tipped off to the Japs' position by Waldron's radioed report, went down on the Jap carriers while the enemy planes refueled and rearmed.

"A PBY picked up Gay the next day."

The attack by Torpedo Squadron Eight from the *Hornet* was not the only fateful attack by U.S. torpedo bombers that day. The same sad fate awaited the torpedo bombers from the *Yorktown* and the *Enterprise* and from Midway itself. But their sacrifices were not in vain. In the confusion created by their suicidal attacks, the American dive-bombers from the carriers and Midway were able to catch the Japanese by surprise. With their antiaircraft fire and fighter protection furiously engaged against the low-flying torpedo planes, the Japanese were unable to protect themselves against the dive-bombers. That first day,, three of the four Japanese carriers involved in the battle –the *Akagi*, the *Kaga*, and the *Soryu*–were sunk. The last remaining Jap carrier, the *Hiryu*, was also badly damaged and was sunk by a destroyer the next day.

In the battle the U.S. carrier *Yorktown* was lost. John Field, Yale 1937, war reporter, interviewed survivors and wrote in *Life* magazine:

"At 11:45 came the announcement: 'Stand by to repel enemy air attack.' The only noise was the noise of the engines, but the ship began heeling over from side to side. She was already dodging enemy planes.

"'Stand by to repel dive-bombing attack.' A deafening blast bounced the decks upward. The ship lurched sideways. Another and another. Then again the deck bounced and there was the crash of flying debris. The ship had been hit. Hell broke loose. The bombs dropped on all sides, one right after the other, uncountable in number. Another hit forward and one amidships. The engines began to whine and their volume diminished. The ship slowed down. More hits and near misses. There was the crashing of metal and the dim cries of wounded men. The AA guns stopped firing. From below, it was difficult to tell whether they had been put out of action. The ship was dead in the water.

"The repair crew opened the door, climbed up to the hangar deck. All was shambles. The decks were a mass of twisted metal and debris. Dead and wounded lay everywhere. Fire parties fought the fires and gradually brought them under control. Electricians rigged up portable lights to illuminate the dark, smoke-filled holes. Engineers worked on the engines. Other men patched the flight deck and began landing the *Yorktown's* planes. Gradually the *Yorktown* got up to 15 knots, but she was still not safe.

"Suddenly the loudspeaker went into action again: 'Stand by to repel air attack.' Below decks, there was a tight feeling in stomachs. Then the AA's broke loose and the Japs were on the *Yorktown* again, this time with torpedo bombers. But the high, satisfying whine of the main engines could no longer be heard. The ship struggled into a starboard turn, but two torpedoes caught her forward. All lights went out. The ship listed rapidly and water ran gurgling across the decks. Another torpedo smacked amidships and again the decks lurched. The engines stopped. The ship was dead, apparently capsizing. The guns were silent.

"Then followed a conference between officers, who decided nothing could be done. 'All right, let's get out.' On the hangar deck the port side was awash. Up forward men climbed down ropes into the water. The wounded went down in wire stretchers. The sea was a mass of bobbing heads. There was little conversation, no hysteria. Destroyers pulled the survivors aboard. Almost everybody was rescued. That night the American battle fleet went on to the west, leaving the mighty 'Y' a ghostly hulk on the horizon.

"But the ship did not sink. In the morning it was decided to put a salvage party aboard to tow her into Pearl Harbor. In the afternoon 141 enlisted men and 31 officers were sent back to the *Yorktown*. Soon three to four degrees of list had been taken off her. Then suddenly at 3:00 P.M. the Japs struck again. This time with torpedoes from submarines. One hit the carrier. Two more hit the destroyer *Hammann*, tied up alongside. The *Hammann* started going down, and its crew and the carrier crew began to abandon ship.

"That night, underneath the stars, were piled dead and wounded bodies. Survivors of the *Yorktown* watched the hulk of their ship still floating through the night. Perhaps she could still be saved? But at dawn, salvage was impossible. The ship had a terrible list to port. Said Captain Buckmaster, 'Her flight deck was in the water. Her battle flags were still flying. We hadn't taken them down."

"At 6:30 A.M. all hands on the destroyers were called on deck. Gradually the *Yorktown* was settling. There was no commotion, no fire. Nobody said anything. Taps sounded out across the water. Sailors, lining the rails, raised their hands in salute. At 7:01 A.M. the *Yorktown* sank. It was June 7, 1942, six months to the hour after the first shot at Pearl Harbor."

The United States had lost the *Yorktown* in the Battle of Midway, but the Japanese had lost all four of their carriers and abandoned their attack. The myth of their invincibility had been shattered. The action off Midway had cost them not only four carriers but a heavy cruiser, the lives of 2,200 sailors, 234 planes, and the best of their naval pilots. The Japanese never again regained the initiative.

On Midway after the battle Paul Rennell wrote his mother and father: "At the time of this writing, the afternoon of my birthday, the trouble is over and we are naturally thrilled at the outcome. The whole thing was as nerve wracking as anything I've ever lived through, but I guess it just wasn't time for my number to come up so I'm able to write this letter. The waiting was the worst part. We knew they were coming ... we were here a week ahead of time ... and these contact reports kept coming in, each one giving a grimmer picture of our chances ... I think I must have lived right to have gotten through the two biggest actions of the war so far. Needless to say, I have had enough ... war is a terrible thing."

War continued to be a terrible thing for Paul and many others. Even though the tide had turned, long years, many battles, and much suffering lay ahead. The men of Yale 1937 would be very much a part of that struggle.

On June 20, 1942, two weeks after Midway and far removed from the battles of the Pacific, a momentous decision was made at Hyde Park, New York, that would ultimately bring an end to the war, and change the whole course of twentieth-century history. On that day President Roosevelt and Prime Minister Winston Churchill made the decision, regardless of cost, to go ahead with the development and production of the atomic bomb. Churchill wrote that the Allies "could not run the mortal risk of being outstripped in this awful sphere." Thus the Manhattan project was born.

(text omitted)

Meanwhile, in the Pacific, the Japanese still had immense naval superiority in battleships, cruisers, and destroyers. The loss of four carriers at Midway temporarily forced them into a defensive strategy, but with their vast gains in the southwest, they could still threaten Australia. To consolidate their holdings, they landed troops in July at

Buna and Gona on Papua (New Guinea) to march over the Owen Stanley Mountains to Port Moresby and hastened to complete the airfield they had started at Guadalcanal in the Solomons. Once finished, the airfield would enable Japan to make a bid for air superiority over the Coral Sea, cut the approaches to Australia, and threaten Fiji and Noumea. To prevent this, the U.S. Navy began plans for its first offensive, and first amphibious operation of the war: the invasion of Guadalcanal and its neighboring small island of Tulagi.

To cover the Guadalcanal landings all the U.S. Navy's remaining naval strength, including four carriers, the *Wasp*, the *Hornet*, the *Saratoga*, and the *Enterprise*, was thrown into the South Pacific.

(text omitted)

The landings at Guadalcanal and Tulagi were at first deceptively easy and gave no indication of the protracted, bitter struggle to come. Under protection from carrier planes and naval bombardment, the Marines walked ashore virtually unopposed on Guadalcanal and against little opposition on Tulagi. On one of the transports Don McNeely watched with amazement to see how easy it seemed. By the next afternoon they had captured the small town on Tulagi and beaten back a Japanese counterattack. On Guadalcanal they had taken the partially finished airstrip and named it Henderson Field. Peterkin's squadron on the *Saratoga* provided air cover, while on the *Enterprise* Fred Mears flew search missions, looking for enemy craft which might try to interrupt the landings.

Suddenly, on the second night of the invasion, everything changed. Already two heavy Japanese air raids had interrupted the landing operations and cost the American carriers one-fifth of their fighters in beating off attacks. As a result, the carriers were pulled out of range of Guadalcanal, leaving the Marines, the transports, and the protecting cruisers without air support. After dark a Japanese cruiser force raced down the so-called Slot, the channel between Santa Isabel and Malaita on the north and New Georgia and Guadalcanal on the south. The volcanic cone of Savo Island obscured its approach, and in the ensuing battle the U.S. Navy received one of its most stunning defeats in all history - four cruisers sunk, another severely damaged. More than 1,000 American sailors lost their lives. The rest of the cruisers and the transports, only partially unloaded, retired on a southeasterly course away from the combat area. The 16,000 Marines on Tulagi and Guadalcanal were left on their own, with less than a month's rations, no heavy weapons, four days' supply of ammunition, and one bulldozer to finish the airfield on which so much of the success of the operation now depended. Fortunately, on August 15 Navy destroyers were able to dash near the beach at night and unload ammunition and fuel oil. Two days later the airstrip was finished, and a flight of Dauntless dive-bombers and twelve fighters landed. Meanwhile, the Japanese had begun to land reinforcements, thus beginning the gradual buildup by both forces, turning what had begun as a minor engagement into one of the crucial battles of the Pacific War.

On August 23-24 a Japanese fleet was discovered steaming south to protect a transport convoy planning to land Japanese marines. The first attack was made from the deck of the U.S. carrier *Saratoga*. While Peterkin' s crew manned the flight deck, keeping things running smoothly, Al Wright took off with his dive-bombing squadron to hit the light carrier *Ryujo*. The Japanese ship was caught refueling her planes, and hits from the U.S. dive-bombers and torpedo planes sent her helplessly circling. She sank four hours later; Al Wright had helped to bag a Japanese carrier.

Meanwhile, on the afternoon of August 24, Fred Mears was out on a search mission but found nothing and was flying back to the *Enterprise* "fat and happy." As he told it, "At five-fifteen we reached the ship, made our recognition signal, and started to approach the carrier. I looked over and saw a cruiser which was smoking.

"All of a sudden a terrific barrage of AA fire burst from all the ships in the force. The battleship accompanying our carrier lit up like a Christmas tree. Black and white puffs of smoke covered the late afternoon sky. Our ships began to turn and their wakes curved boiling out behind them.

"I looked up and saw three Jap dive-bombers, one behind the other, diving on our carrier. I heard on the air: 'All friendly planes keep clear during the attack.' ... I saw a mass of flame–a plane burning fiercely–flutter down like a butterfly and kiss the water. Shrapnel was falling in patches on the ocean like heavy rain. Bombs struck the sea near us and made dirty brown circles in the water...

"At six-fifteen we received word to jettison our bombs and land.. . . When I landed, half the flight deck aft was blown up by a bomb hit. The plane handler who taxied me up the deck had a bandage around his head under his helmet. Everybody looked tired. Being aboard a ship when it's a bombing target is one of the most terrifying experiences there is. There are no foxholes on a carrier.

A couple of days later our skipper called together the eight of us torpedo pilots who were left on the carrier and told us we would fly the remaining planes off the deck in the morning. The ship was bound for port to be repaired."

Meanwhile, the *Saratoga* had weathered what came to be called the Battle of the Eastern Solomons. In addition to sinking the *Ryujo*, Peterkin's and Wright's planes had attacked enemy cruisers and destroyers, scoring some hits and near misses but sinking none.

But disaster was near for the *Saratoga*. On August 31 a Japanese submarine trailing her sent a torpedo deep into her engine room. She could no longer get up enough speed to launch her planes and she too would have to return to dry dock for repairs.

Peterkin, Wright, and also McNeely, who had now boarded the ship, were given their instructions: all planes were to be flown off, and the officers and crew were to take with them only what they were wearing. To help the planes get airborne, the cruiser *Minneapolis* attached a long towline to the *Saratoga's* bow and pulled the disabled carrier at a speed sufficient to allow the planes to be airborne. They flew off to Espiritu Santo in the New Hebrides. There they met up with Fred Mears and his group. Torpedo Eight was reborn, this time in a jungle camp.

Fred wrote: "I had known most of the men in Larsen's detachment of Torpedo Eight for a short time after Midway.... When we got to the squadron camp on the hill behind the field, we found the members of Torpedo Eight busy clearing away brush and burning it, pitching their tents, and setting up cots covered with mosquito netting.... We dug our own latrine and we built our own shower by pulling two oil barrels full of water on top of a log stand we had erected. Lt. Benny Grosscup, who was one of the eleven iron men of the Yale football team that beat Princeton in 1934 with no substitutions, directed these activities.... There were two other Yale AVS officers in the squadron: Lt. George Flinn, who directed the paperwork of Torpedo Eight with meticulous efficiency, and DeWitt Peterkin, Jr., the engineering officer, who was responsible for keeping most of the planes in the air most of the time."

Henry Salomon, in his television series and book, *Victory at Sea*, wrote about Guadalcanal: "For the next six months there was fighting by land, sea, and air, as terrible as any ever recorded in the annals of war, over that smoothed-out scrap of earth on the rim of that reeking island.

"Guadalcanal stank. Its jungle was the type known as 'rain forest' and the porous earth with its lush decaying vegetation gave off a sour, disgusting smell. The damp air never seemed to stir and hung hot and fetid and almost palpable, hospitable only to malarial fevers and creeping rot. Underfoot slithered jungle rats and three-foot lizards, and from overhead dropped insatiable leeches that fixed themselves wetly on human skin and sucked."

In this tropical hell the land battle swayed back and forth; the Japanese determined to retake Henderson Field and drive the Marines into the sea. In the Battle of "Bloody Ridge" on September 12, suicidal banzai charges brought them to within 1,000 yards of the runway before they were driven back, leaving behind over 600 dead.

The Americans counterattacked, sometimes in force, more often in small patrols, company size. John Hersey, a war correspondent for *Time* magazine, had graduated from Yale just a year before 1937, and he was a friend of many of the men of 1937 who were on that island at that time. In one of the most memorable books of World War II, *Into the Valley*, Hersey tells of accompanying a Marine Corps unit trying to force a crossing of a small stream four miles west of Henderson Field and of the failure of that mission in an ambush set up by the Japanese. In one of his more eloquent passages Hersey describes the American Marines of his company, all of whom knew they faced a high probability of death in those dark jungles of Guadalcanal. "They were just American boys. They did not want that valley, or any part of its jungle. They were ex grocery clerks, ex-highway laborers, ex-bank clerks, ex-schoolboys, boys with a clean record and maybe a little extra restlessness, but not killers.

They had volunteered; they had come into the Marines with their eyes open. Yes, but they had joined the Marines to see the world, or to get away from a guilt, or most likely to escape the draft, not knowingly to kill or be killed.

"It would be unfair to say that there was fear on any single one of those faces. But neither was there elation. There certainly was weariness ... these boys had arrived on August 7 and this day was October 8, and every inch of the Guadalcanal beachhead had been front lines all along.. . . There was also hunger visible there... .

"But the truth on those faces was not just a physical thing. It was some shadow out of the mind, an uneasiness. It was a positive sign that if some lieutenant colonel had come up and given them their choice between going into that valley or going home, they would have said the hell with the valley."

On and near Henderson Field, without control of the air or the sea, the Marines and the Navy fliers were subjected to days and weeks and months of bombardment by Japanese planes and ships. The Japanese Navy filtered more and more men ashore, and each night its ships churned down the Slot to bombard the American positions with everything up to sixteen-inch guns. Deep foxholes offered the only partial safety. On the very day that the Marines stopped the enemy on Bloody Ridge, the U.S. aircraft carrier *Wasp* was sunk by a Japanese submarine. With the *Saratoga* and the *Enterprise* under repair, this left only one U.S. carrier, the *Hornet*, in the Pacific. The men on Guadalcanal–and Henderson Field–were even more exposed to the enemy. Salomon wrote: "Before the year was out half a hundred ships, Allied and Japanese–carriers, cruisers, battleships, destroyers, transports, submarines–were stricken from the naval lists.

In the air, pilots on both sides died by day and by night to protect the ships on one hand and destroy them on the other. Success on Guadalcanal depended on whether the supply ships got through."

This was the base - this was Henderson Field–to which Fred Mears and DeWitt Peterkin and the rest of Torpedo Eight were now assigned–also Al Wright and Don McNeely. Bob Heinl described the field as alternately transformed from "a bowl of black dust which fouled up airplane engines" to a "quagmire of black mud which made takeoff resemble nothing more than a fly trying to rise from a runway of molasses." This was where Peterkin spent the rest of August, September, October, and up to the middle of November, It was such difficult and dangerous duty that only half of the squadron stayed on Guadalcanal while the other half got some rest at Espiritu Santo. But Pete, being engineering officer, whose job it was to keep as many planes fit for combat as possible, stayed there all the time, got no relief. The waking hours were difficult; sleep impossible. 'We didn't have many surface ships," he reported. "The Japs came down the Slot every night–cruisers and battleships. If they didn't find any surface ships to attack, they would unload on us in our foxholes on the beach or near the field. Actually, the armor-piercing shells were not as bad as the bombardment shells. They didn't spread as far. In the daytime we used a tent next to Henderson Field and worked to fix up the only TBFs in that part of the world."

On October 3 Fred Mears, with his gunner, Hicks, and his bombardier, Deitsch, took one of the few remaining TBFs off from Henderson Field to attack a Japanese cruiser and two destroyers, reported to be 150 miles west of the Slot. He was loaded with four 500-pound bombs instead of a torpedo. "We caught sight of the ships sooner than we had expected. They were in line with one destroyer leading and one trailing the cruiser.... The dive-bombers dove first on the cruiser, from about 9,000 feet.... I glided down to get into position. I saw a near miss off the stern of the cruiser as I pushed into about a sixty-degree dive.... I was intent on fixing my point of aim ... the bow of the big cruiser ahead of me. I pressed the bomb release three times and pulled up. I glanced at my altimeter. I was at 2,000 feet.

"Close to port I saw a float biplane closing on us, and I kicked into a turn away from him. Then I felt the vibration of the turret gun firing, and Hicks told me over the interphone that he had shot him down.

"I circled on down past a destroyer ahead of the cruiser. We were only 800 yards from the cruiser and Hicks was strafing the deck. As we went past they were firing at us and I could see the bullets sprinkling in the water like rain. Suddenly they found our range, and I could see traces looping into us. Then I felt a blow like something had slapped us on the tail.

"Hicks cried, 'Mr. Mears! Deitsch has been hit. I think we are hit badly!' I turned and fled along the water.... I got into Henderson just at twilight and we rushed Deitsch to the hospital. The doctor said he had three pieces of shrapnel in his brain and gave him little chance to live.

"Peterkin' s engineers, who looked at the plane the next day, found only three control wires holding the flipper and three the rudder. There was a hole you could put your head through where a 20-millimeter shell had hit the bomber's compartment and exploded inside and perhaps twenty other holes in the tail of the fuselage, made by explosive bullets."

Flying for Torpedo Eight was brought to an abrupt halt on October 13. That day marked the beginning of Japan's biggest drive to recapture Guadalcanal. The Japanese concentrated four battleships, five carriers, ten cruisers, and twenty-nine destroyers to land reinforcements and put Henderson Field out of action. At one o'clock in the afternoon, twenty-seven Japanese bombers placed their loads squarely on the U.S. plane parking area. An hour and a half later twelve more bombers came over and hit the same target. Only two U.S. torpedo planes were in flying condition after that raid.

The night was much worse. Two Japanese battleships, the *Kongo* and the *Haruma*, along with cruisers and destroyers, stood out in Ironbottom Sound (so called for the number of ships which had been sunk in it) and lobbed their shells onto Henderson. Fred described it: "Coconut trees split off and crashed to the ground, shrapnel whirred through the air. We smelled the powder of detonating shells. The sky was now ghostly, now brilliant with fires and with pinwheel star shells.

'We climbed out of our foxholes, intent on evacuating our camp area, which was being so heavily shelled. We were piling into a large truck to go to the big bomb shelters near the beach. Men were yelling, even crying, and trying to hide behind one another or force their way to the bottom of the truck. Some held their shirts overhead as though for protection. We passed the hospital near the campus area and could see the doctors operating in the midst of shell fire.

"The truck halted directly behind the gun position at which the Japs were shooting. We poured out the back and streamed off into the woods toward the bomb shelters, flattening out or leaping into ditches when we saw a glitter to seaward."

The next day the pilots and crewmen of Torpedo Eight returned to their camp area to survey the damage. All the few remaining planes had been hit, and none was flyable. The camp was a mess, completely destroyed.

Fred wrote: "We decided to abandon our camp area and move back with the Marines near the front lines. We issued all the squadron guns and ammunition to the men and then, taking only the belongings and supplies we could carry, we moved to the hills and settled in a gully with a Marine special-weapons unit. We were prepared to break up into parties of eight and strike off into the hills if the Japs should make a landing and take the island."

Even in this desperate situation, DeWitt Peterkin and his engineering crew still kept trying to keep the planes in working order. There were three TBFs which they thought could be repaired, the least-damaged one in about a week. Continually exposed to Japanese artillery fire during daylight, and with almost no sleep at night, they labored to get one of the planes airworthy. By October 22 they had succeeded. Skipper Larsen took it up for a test hop, and the squadron began using it to bomb Japanese artillery emplacements on the island. But the plane did not last long. The next day it was shot down and landed in the sea. The pilot and the two crew members swam to shore, but a Marine major, who had gone along just for the fun of it, was drowned.

In those dark days it seemed as if our Guadalcanal invasion would end in failure. It certainly looked that way to Pete and Fred and their squadron mates. On the very night the squadron lost its last plane the Japanese started a land drive to recapture Henderson Field and drive them into the sea. They slept under the continuous chatter and barking of machine guns, rifles, mortar and howitzer fire, and the booming and pounding of bigger guns. Snipers were everywhere, day and night, in the trees hanging in baskets or stretched along limbs, often disguised with coconut coats and hats. Zeros were continually overhead, stunting over Henderson. The bombing seemed never to stop.

But the Marines, fighting to hold the island, and later the Army infantrymen who relieved them, were not about to surrender. Under the jungle conditions, the privations, and the terrible danger, the U.S. soldiers hardened into formidable veterans who could match the Japanese trick for trick, skill for skill.

And there *were* U.S. planes, too, even if all Torpedo Eight's were gone. Henderson Field was gradually built up; bombers from carriers and Flying Fortresses from land bases fought Zeros and made attacks on enemy transports and warships. The surface Navy tangled with Japanese forces in the Battle of Santa Cruz Island on October 26. By then the repaired but still battered *Enterprise* had returned to action to give support to the *Hornet*, which was attempting to prevent the landing of Japanese troops. In the ensuing action the *Hornet* was sunk. Lt. James Day, Yale 1937, was on the communications staff of the *Hornet* that day. His assignment was to decode messages and to act as assistant signal officer. He described what happened: "We had been trailed all night by a Japanese submarine which surfaced at dawn and radioed our exact position. When the bombing attack came, I was fortunately not on the signal bridge, having been detached from there at general quarters to be the communicator for the executive officer in the after part of the- island. You can't see anything from there, but we heard a terrible racket as the bombs hit, then a blast as a plane hit the signal bridge. Even where we were, the heat was intense.

"After the first wave, fires broke out all over the ship, but everything seemed to be brought under control. Damage control was marvelous. But what did us in was a torpedo in the engine room. This took away our power to move. We were dead in the water, a sitting duck for another attack. The exec tried to get a tow from the cruiser *Northampton*, but this was unsuccessful and the line parted. More attacks followed. Our communications division lost nine signalmen. We couldn't do any signaling. The flagstaffs were all messed up and hanging loose. It was dreadful–nine bodies around...

"I was ordered to help secure the coding vault and lock it because we were going to abandon ship. We went below decks, but we couldn't lock the vault because the bombing had sprung the door. Therefore, all code publications, to protect secrecy, had to be put in leaded bags and thrown overboard.

"After doing that, I was on my own. Everybody was going overboard. We had a big list to starboard. Some people went over to starboard, but most went down the port side, the longest way to the water. It was a hell of a long drop. I had a terrible fear I wasn't going to latch on to a line. But the Lord was with me. I'd shirked the abandon-ship drill back in Pearl Harbor, and I'd never gone down a line in my life. Yet I was one of the few people who made it down without a scratch. When I finally got to the water, a great sense of relief spread over me.... I struck out toward the destroyer *Morris* and swam there in maybe 25 minutes. They pulled me up and I was safe."

Although the *Hornet* was gone, the Japanese were again turned back in their attempts to land reinforcements on Guadalcanal. Clearly they were no longer able to sustain the attrition of experienced air crews which the fighting was causing, nor the losses among their surface ships. This was especially true after the last and most significant of all the Guadalcanal sea and air battles: the Battle of Guadalcanal, November 13, 14, and 15. The opening rounds of this engagement went to the Japanese as the American cruisers, the *Atlanta* and the *Juneau*, were sunk and the *San Francisco* was badly damaged, but by the end of the third day the Japanese were in full withdrawal, having lost two battleships, a heavy cruiser, three destroyers, and eleven transports.

* That summer and fall the USS *Alchiba*, a supply ship, was busy running supplies to the Marines on Guadalcanal. On the morning of November 28 she was torpedoed off Lunga Point. The crew, among them Navigator Edward Schroeder, Yale *1937*, moved ashore, then returned to the ship to refloat her, patch her up, and make the run back to San Francisco on her own bottom. The *Alchiba* and her crew were awarded the Presidential Unit Citation, the only supply ship to be so honored.

Gradually the Americans got in more supplies; gradually there were more and newer planes, and new pilots and crews. The Japanese began to retreat as their supplies and reinforcements were choked off. The end came on February 3, 1943, when the few remaining Japanese evacuated the island. The American commanding general was able to report to Allied Headquarters: "Total and complete defeat of Japanese forces on Guadalcanal effected 1625 today."

By then Fred Mears and DeWitt Peterkin had left the island. Skipper Larsen and the last three pilots of Torpedo Squadron Eight were relieved by a marine torpedo squadron on November 15. Fred had left before and was soon on a transport headed for San Francisco. Pete's departure was more dramatic. It came immediately after the big American naval victory of November 14-15, and he was the first naval officer to be flown back to Hawaii to give a personal report. When his plane landed, Adm. John Towers himself, commander of Naval Air Forces, was waiting to greet him. Pete was told to report immediately to Pearl Harbor, where an admiral's barge was waiting to take him to see Adm. Chester Nimitz, commander in chief of U.S. Naval Forces in the Pacific. Pete was ushered into a room "completely circled with generals and admirals. I was seated on a stool in the middle of the room and interrogated for an hour. I remember being asked 'What do we need most down there?' I answered, learn how to build revetments.' These are three-sided shelters which can be built out of palm trees and would protect the planes from shrapnel during bombardments. We had probably lost more planes on the ground in Guadalcanal than in the air."

As Pete left the room, he heard one admiral ask another, "What class at the Academy was that young man?" Peter figured there could be no better compliment offered for his performance than that question.

He was also lionized by the press. The Associated Press reported from Pearl Harbor that "Lieutenant DeWitt Peterkin, Jr., first American naval officer to arrive here from the Solomons since the Navy's victory on November 14-15, said he believed some 10,000 Japanese have been killed on Guadalcanal. 'The Marines and other forces felt better after last week's big naval battle than any time since I was there,' said Lieutenant Peterkin of New York, an assistant to the J. P. Morgan partners before he entered the service." Frank Tremaine of the United Press reported that Peterkin said that the Japanese were suffering more heavy casualties in their attempt to wrest Henderson Field from American hands. "The sight of a prisoner," Pete was quoted, "was an oddity. Almost no prisoners are taken on either side."

Fred Mears did not survive the war. He was killed when his plane crashed and burned near the Mexican border during bombing practice on June 26, 1943. His ashes were flown to sea with an aerial escort.

Posthumously he was awarded the Distinguished Flying Cross. The citation read: "For heroism and extraordinary achievement in aerial combat against enemy forces in the Solomon Islands on October 3 and 5, 1942. Participating in a raid launched by three torpedo bombers against a force of hostile warships proceeding toward Guadalcanal, Lieutenant Mears, boldly striking at the enemy with four 500-pound bombs, contributed to the aggregate score of two direct hits which set a Japanese cruiser aflame and one near miss on a destroyer. When he returned to strafe the cruiser, an enemy shell burst ripped a hole in the fuselage of his plane and critically wounded his bomber. Two days later he took off on a flight of five bombers, twelve scout bombers, and one Flying Fortress to raid Rekata Bay on Santa Isabel Island. As one of the nine surviving planes to reach their objectives, Lieutenant Mears ... vigorously strafed Japanese ground installations in the face of tremendous fire from both enemy aircraft and shore batteries. By his aggressive fighting spirit and skillful airmanship on these two flights, he enabled his gunners to shoot down a total of three planes."

A reviewer in the *New York Times* commented on Fred Mears' book, *Carrier Combat:* "In straight prose he tells of the hellish fighting at Guadalcanal and other murderous battles of the South Pacific. The mind cannot comprehend the crazy irrationality of the naked facts and they seem unreal. Mears himself offers no comment. He looks out upon the beauty of sea and sky and sunset, describes the poker games, the electrifying battle orders, the pursuit of girls, the dog-eared prayer book and the farewell letter by a dead flyer. These are simple facts.... Call it heroism, but read this moving book and savor something beyond all heroism."